EXPERIENCE THE POWER

Messages On 12
Steps Of Faith

BY JOHN TERRY

C.S.S Publishing Co., Inc.
Lima, Ohio

EXPERIENCE THE POWER:
MESSAGES ON 12 STEPS OF FAITH

Copyright © 1992 by
The C.S.S. Publishing Company, Inc.
Lima, Ohio

Library of Congress Cataloging-in-Publication Data

Terry, John, 1943-
    Experience the power : messages on 12 steps of faith / by John Terry.
        p.   cm.
    ISBN 1-55673-360-7
    1. Twelve-step programs — Sermons.   2. Sermons, American.
I. Title
BV4316.A37T47   1992
248.9'6—dc20   91-23971
                                                                      CIP

9214 / ISBN 1-55673-360-7   PRINTED IN U.S.A.

To Elise,
whose faith journey
has illuminated my own.

Table of Contents

Step One — Honesty   9
    Proverbs 23:29-35
    Romans 7:15-24
    Luke 8:26-39

Step Two — Hope   17
    Isaiah 12:1-6
    2 Corinthians 12:7-10
    Mark 10:46-52

Step Three — Faith   25
    Isaiah 55:6-9
    Hebrews 11:1-7
    Matthew 8:5-13

Step Four — Courage   33
    Psalm 139:1-6
    Acts 9:1-9
    Matthew 26:69-75

Step Five — Integrity   41
    Isaiah 6:1-8
    1 John 1:5-10
    John 4:16-24

Step Six — Willingness   47
    Isaiah 1:12-20
    Hebrews 4:14-16
    John 5:2-9a

Step Seven — Humility   55
    Psalm 51:1-14
    2 Timothy 2:20-26
    Matthew 23:25-36

Step Eight — Love   63
    Psalm 19:7-13
    2 Corinthians 5:16-21
    Matthew 7:7-14

Step Nine — Discipline   69
    Numbers 5:5-10
    Ephesians 4:25-32
    Matthew 5:21-26

Step Ten — Perseverence   77
    Psalm 15:1-5
    1 Corinthians 10:1-13
    Luke 12:42-48

Step Eleven — Spirituality   85
    Psalm 25:1-15
    1 Thessalonians 5:12-22
    Matthew 26:36-46

Step Twelve — Responsibility   93
    Isaiah 61:1-4
    Galatians 6:1-10
    Luke 19:1-10

Introduction

I did not mean to write this book. It is the by-product of my preparation for a conference I was hosting.

From 1986 to 1989, I was the chaplain of Laurel Heights Hospital, an adolescent treatment center in Atlanta, Georgia. The administrator, Terry Robinson, had asked me to prepare some educational opportunities for local clergy.

As I sorted about for an appropriate topic related both to the concerns clergy face and to the work that hospital was doing, it occurred to me that treatment for alcohol and drug addiction is something about which clergy should be well educated. However, most of us clergy are terribly ignorant about addiction and treatment.

My seminary education in the field of alcoholism consisted of a brief talk in a pastoral counseling class, after which we were given material, written in the mid-1950s, explaining alcoholism to clergy. My continuing education on the subject consisted of a talk I heard in 1971 titled "The Alcoholic and His Wife." The assumption seemed to be that alcoholics are adult males.

For me to host a workshop for clergy on addiction, I felt I needed to develop a much greater understanding of the subject for myself. As a way of doing this, I decided to preach a series of 12 sermons on the 12 steps of Alcoholics Anonymous.

I began to search the book stores of Atlanta for help. The religious book stores had very little material on addiction and recovery, especially in understanding the spiritual dimension of these steps. The secular book stores had a lot of books on addiction. There were even some books that dealt with "spirituality," but it was a kind of generic spirituality. I found nothing that set these steps within our biblical tradition.

With fear and trembling, I launched into the 12-week series. It was clear from the beginning of the first sermon that something was happening in the congregation. I feared there would be too much discomfort with the subject. But that was not the case. There developed an intensive receptivity within the congregation that I had never felt before.

It was as though folks had been waiting to hear about this path to recovery but had been afraid to ask. While I do not normally print copies of my sermons, I was asked for more and more copies. Some took copies and told me about a family member who was struggling with addiction or had achieved sobriety. Others were interested for themselves.

Sometime after I preached this series, and after I conducted two other workshops on addiction for religious leaders, I happened to be sitting at lunch with a representative of a company that publishes books for addiction treatment professionals. He asked if I had written anything in which his company might be interested. I mentioned this series of sermons. After looking at what I had written, he asked to publish them. There seems to be no other comparable work in print.

I declined the offer, because as I thought about what I had done, I came to believe that this is most needed within the church. These certainly are not the best sermons I have ever preached. I hope others are moved to do a similar series to improve on this modest effort. The problem of chemical abuse directly or indirectly effects one person in three. We need to expand.

This kind of reflection on addiction and recovery is most needed within the community of faith, because it is our faith that has what we need to lead us in a healthy journey through life. As we struggle to get from where we are to where God would have us go, these are the steps to bring us back home.

These 12 steps are clearly a journey of faith. It is a faith journey that is best traveled when the guideposts of Scripture lead us on the way. In the struggle against addiction, the church should provide those to whom it ministers the powerful resources of our faith.

STEP ONE — HONESTY

Proverbs 23:29-35
Romans 7:15-24
Luke 8:26-39

This past summer I read an article that caused me to make a significant change from my usual practice of preaching from the lectionary. The article, titled, "Coming to Grips with Drug Abuse," made the point that neither clergy nor parents need to be experts on drug dependency, though we do need to be well informed. We need to understand what it means to describe chemical dependency as a disease. Therefore I am going to talk about addiction for a time before I talk about today's Scripture readings.

But what is most important for the church to understand is that the Christian faith is the spiritual foundation on which recovery is built. The Christian faith is the source of strength and self-esteem which will help keep us from self-destructive behavior. There are 12 steps commonly used in this process, returning us from exile. The exile may have been the result of chemical abuse or the abuse of food. It may have come as a result of an inability to control emotions or an inability to control sexual behavior.

For the purpose of this sermon, we will consider substance abuse as a paradigm of life out of control, which is in exile from its true nature and destiny. No one seeks to become an addict. Those who become chemically dependent are seeking things that we all seek. And like all of us, they often are seeking in the wrong places or by the wrong means.

Experts on adolescent chemical dependency and other youth problems repeatedly explain drug abuse by pointing to adolescents' lack of self-esteem and feeling of powerlessness.

A shy teenager takes his or her first drink or drug and suddenly becomes the life of the party. Another, who has trouble controlling his or her emotions, finds that a joint, pill or drink brings a feeling of omnipotence.

People drink and use drugs because that fixes whatever is wrong — if only momentarily — and it works quickly. The effect of this momentary cure is especially powerful for the young person who is biochemically prone to chemical dependency.

Addiction appears to be an inherited trait, just like inheriting the color of our eyes or the shape of our noses. That could help explain why two people consuming exactly the same amount of alcohol have such different reactions: one becomes relaxed; the other goes out of control. For those prone to chemical dependency by genetics and/or environment, though they may pay a price for the abuse, the positive effects they feel from drug and alcohol use can be seen to far outweigh the negative effects.

However, as tolerance for the drug (an early sign of chemical dependency) grows, so does drug use. In time, the positive side of the drug experience wanes and pain begins to take over. What is the answer to the pain but more of the same fix? Life becomes more and more unpredictable, but the drug remains predictable — at least in its immediate effects.

When our life is unmanageable, drugs and alcohol are two of the great illusion builders that fool us into thinking that for a time we are in control, while all the time making us more out of control.

Eventually the person reaches a point of despair in which he or she experiences powerlessness in a way that even the alcohol and drug cannot fix. This is the moment when many seek outside help. Others simply surrender to their dependency.

These steps begin with a frank admission of powerlessness over one's addiction. It is the spiritual basis for the 12-step recovery program. This spiritual journey is the only effective long-term program that works in keeping chemically addicted people sober and functioning. Ironically, addiction is basically a medical problem for which the only effective, long-term cure is spiritual.

In the article to which I referred earlier, the author made these points about youth, though they are true for all ages: "I have often thought that if only parents, the church and society would teach children the basic spiritual truths centered in these 12 steps, we could save them from much pain and give them something to say 'Yes' to."

This sermon is the first of 12 which focus on the 12 steps. Steps one and 12 talk specifically about drinking. Steps two through 11 do not. The 12 steps make more reference to explicit and implicit spiritual issues than to substance abuse. This sermon is going to look at substance abuse that makes life uncontrollable, and at a biblical basis for understanding that experience.

Let me issue two disclaimers. While I am strongly against the use of any illegal drug, these will not be lectures advocating abstinence from alcohol, except for those for whom total abstinence is appropriate. I believe in temperance. That is not the same as abstinence. Also, I am not trying to do a Sunday morning therapy session. For those who need it, there is no substitute for being a part of Alcoholics Anonymous, or any other appropriate 12-step group. These sermons are not primarily focusing on substance abuse. What I will do in these 12 sermons is look at the scriptural basis for the 12 steps.

What do you need to know is these 12 steps, which were originated by Alcoholics Anonymous, are now used by close to 200 other 12-step groups. The same basic principles apply to whatever it is that makes your life unmanageable.

A.A. literature includes a disclaimer that says the material is not the property of any one religion, and that is true. But you should also know that historically, the 12 steps came out of the Christian church, and whether anyone admits it or not, the stuff that makes it work is the stuff of the Christian faith.

Step one, we admitted we were powerless over alcohol and other drugs, that our lives had become unmanageable.

11

The first text we examine as our biblical basis and spiritual resource is Proverbs 23:29-35. There are a lot of folks who say that religious folks lead sheltered lives. But listen to this description of a life that has become unmanageable, and see if it does not indicate some firsthand experience:

> *"Show me someone who drinks too much, who has to try out fancy drinks, and I will show you someone miserable and sorry for himself, always complaining. His eyes are bloodshot, and he has bruises that could have been avoided. Don't let wine tempt you, even though it is rich red, and it sparkles in the cup, and it goes down smoothly.*
>
> *"The next morning you will feel as if you have been bitten by a poisonous snake. Weird sights will appear before your eyes, and you will not be able to think or speak clearly. You will feel as if you were out on the ocean, seasick, swinging high up in the rigging of a tossing ship. 'I must have been hit,' you will say; 'I must have been beaten up, but I don't remember it. Why can't I wake up? I need another drink.' "*

Or *The Anchor Bible* also puts it with clarity:

> *"Those who linger over wine,*
> *Who drain the mixing bowl.*
> *Afterward it will bite like a snake,*
> *It secretes the venom of a viper;*
> *Your eyes will see strange apparitions,*
> *And your mind and speech will be confused;*
> *You will be like one prostrate far at sea,*
> *(Or) who rolls drunkenly like the top of the mast,*
> *(Saying) 'They hit me but it didn't hurt!*
> *They beat me but I didn't know it!*
> *As soon as I can wake up*
> *I shall want another drink!' "*

This almost humorous description of a hangover sounds like something Bill Cosby could have written. Its presence in

Holy Scripture means that God understands us when we reach the point in our life when we are powerless to do anything about our condition. When we find our life unmanageable, God understands, and the saints of the church speak to our condition.

The message here is not abstinence, but temperance. It talks of how wine in excess leads to other problems, such as fighting, promiscuity and crime. That was what the Bible said thousands of years ago, and it has not changed. God understood and understands.

This ancient scripture recognizes the connection of substance abuse — then that was just wine — and personal economic ruin. Proverbs also says (23:19ff *Anchor Bible*):

Hear now, my son, and gain wisdom,
  Give attention to following the right path;
  Be not of those who drink wine to excess,
  For the heavy drinker and the glutton will be disinherited,
    And sleep will clothe a man in rags.

Let me say something here that is very important to know and understand. Recently I was asked why, if alcohol causes so much trouble, God created it. Wine in Israel was a sign of the blessing of God and was to be used as a way of exemplifying the meaning of this blessing.

To make drinking an end in itself, and simply a means of self-indulgence, is to invite disasters. Wine must assist one in living life. To use it as an escape from the living of life is to make it an enemy.

There is a very interesting passage in the book of Ecclesiasticus or The Wisdom of Jesus the Son of Sirach. It is a Holy writing that was written a century or two before the birth of Christ and is considered by some as a Scripture. Remember this was written before the understanding that addiction to alcohol and drugs may be genetic. This passage does not take that into account, but it does give theological understanding to God's purpose in creating wine.

Do not aim to be valiant over wine,
   for wine has destroyed many.
Fire and water prove the temper of steel,
   so wine tests hearts in the strife of the proud.
Wine is like life to men,
   If you drink it in moderation.
What is life to a man which is out of wine?
   It has been created to make men glad.
Wine drunk in season and temperately
   is rejoicing of heart and gladness of soul.
Wine drunk to excess is bitterness of soul,
   with provocation and stumbling.
Drunkenness increases the anger of a fool to his injury,
   reducing his strength and adding wounds (31:25-30).

Does not God understand? Unfortunately, the basic approach coming out of the religious community is to tell those for whom drinking is a problem or those who drink at all, "You are a sinner. Stop it." That is not very helpful. If drinking has made your life unmanageable, then how can you manage to stop? You only make a person feel worse by calling him a sinner for failing to do the impossible. To the guilt is added shame.

What we need to have is spiritual understanding of what is happening to us when life becomes unmanageable. There is no better passage in Scripture or any book on psychology than what St. Paul wrote to the church in Rome. "I do not understand my own actions. For I do not do what I want, but I do the very thing I hate."

Paul talks about the civil war that rages within us, our helplessness in attempting to live up to God's requirements. It is the person who has experienced God's free grace and forgiveness who is the most acutely aware of his own sin and plight.

St. Augustine said, "I do not understand how this very thing for which I lust becomes more delightful when it is forbidden." And again, ". . . this law of sin which was present in the members of even the great apostles is forgiven in baptism, but it does not come to an end."

The cry, "Who will deliver me from this body of death?" is part of the human condition. God understood and understands. The gift of faith is to be able to say with Paul, "Thanks be to God through Jesus Christ our Lord." He was talking about the experience of turning his life over to the power of Christ.

Paul talks about our struggle, but he is not talking about our despair. This step is not a statement of hopelessness. It is a statement of honesty. The good news is that reaching the bottom, we are stripped of our illusions about ourselves and our strength. Knowing that I am not able to manage my life by myself, I am ready to receive help that I would not have if I still had illusions about self-control.

It is often only when we find ourselves crying out as did Paul, with life out of control, that we become ready to receive the One who makes life manageable.

Then there is the rather strange gospel story. I am not going to explain how Jesus sent the demons into the pigs and all that was described in the gospel story. What we can say is that the man described is one whose life was clearly out of control. Most of us manage to carry on with life; at least we do so outwardly.

The man here described in Luke would in the 1960s be in a psychiatric hospital or, today, a street person. What we also know is the reaction of people to this man who was, as the text says, "clothed and in his rightful mind." The reaction of the people? They were afraid.

There is a long and tragic history of people having the town drunk and the village idiot. There is often what is known as "codependency," that is, family and friends who help a person just enough to let him maintain an unmanageable life, but in truth they do not have him healed.

It can be nice to have someone to laugh at, someone to make fun of, someone who makes you feel so much better by comparison. It can be nice to have a friend who is always ready to have one drink too many, to bet too much at a game of poker, to go out looking to cheat on a spouse. That person's

return to spiritual and emotional health is by many unwel-
comed, even feared.

This leads us to the hope-filled words of step two, "Came
to believe that a power greater than ourselves could restore
us to sanity."

In summary, let me say that it is the very experience of this
civil war that rages within us, of knowing what we should do
but being unable to do so, that can be the foundation on which
grows a faith which says with St. Paul, "Wretched person that
I am! Who will deliver me from this body of death? Thanks
be to God through Jesus Christ our Lord!"

STEP TWO — HOPE

Isaiah 12:1-6
2 Corinthians 12:7-10
Mark 10:46-52

Step two. "Came to believe that a power greater than ourselves could restore us to sanity." One word sometimes used to summarize this step is the word *hope*.

We are going to look at today's texts as they relate to believing God restores us as we turn our lives over to that Power greater than ourselves. In the Old Testament reading, Isaiah sings a song of deliverance. The words might sound like a call for personal deliverance, but it is really a song for the deliverance of the nation and a call for a reunited world.

The nation of Israel had suffered terrible disasters at the hands of the Assyrian army, suffering that Israel understood to be the judgment of God. This is a God whose anger is justified. There is, nevertheless, a future in which there is still hope.

That is because God's anger is a loving anger rather than a vengeful anger. God punishes as a loving, not vengeful, parent. This is a God who still refreshes those who come to the well to drink. It was the time of trouble that led God's people to the willingness to stop drinking from their own well and seek to drink from God's. It was a disaster — in this case a national disaster — that convinced them they could no longer depend long on their own power but had to depend on that power of God's which is so much higher.

They were pushed to rely on God because their national life was unmanageable. That seems to be what it takes for humankind to turn things over to God. The more confident we become of our own power, the less inclined we are to remember and give thanks to God.

Consider the contrast between Narcissus, the Greek and Roman mythical character, and Isaiah, the prophet of God. Narcissus saw himself in a pond. He was so infatuated with his reflection that he desired to grasp it and hold on to it. The only way for him to do this was to open his arms and reach for the reflection in the water. In doing so, he fell into the pond and was drowned. So wrapped up with himself, he lost himself.

By contrast, Isaiah envisions a well of life as a well of God's saving favor. Instead of plunging himself into his own reflection, he draws up the water he had received from God's bounty. He had forgotten himself, thrown himself upon the grace of God, and enjoyed the water of salvation.

He said that "The Lord is my strength and my song . . ." I want to do a little celebration here in music as a way of getting us in touch with that higher power.

Music was a major factor in redeeming the church during the Reformation. Martin Luther wrote that the study of music was second only to the study of theology. And when Geneva was besieged and every man was required to stand his turn at guard duty, John Calvin excused only one person from such duty. His name was Louis Bourgeois, the teacher of music to the children, who composed "Old Hundredth," our doxology tune. A Methodist bishop once said more people had been "sung" into his church than came in any other way.

A national disaster and an understanding that the nation would only be redeemed if it drew its strength from a judging, loving and forgiving God was what led Isaiah to faith. By contrast, the gospel story tells of an individual whose personal troubles led him to faith.

The scene is set in Jericho, about 15 miles from Jerusalem. It was just before holy week, as Jesus and the disciples were traveling to Jerusalem.

Here we meet Bartimaeus. It is possible that this is a man who was without health or wealth or social position. He did not even have a name. Bartimaeus means, "son of Timaeus." He was simply identified by who his father was. In those days parents did not name a child unless they wanted to keep the child and assume responsibility for the child's care.

A child who was born with a handicap was often left unnamed and, thereby, unclaimed. Since the only name given us for this blind man means "son of Timaeus," it is possible that no one — not even his parents — had cared about him.

Blindness was common in Palestine. There were no social agencies to help. The blind had to beg or die. The blind and lame often posted themselves at the city gateway, especially at Passover season.

It was then the custom that a distinguished rabbi on a journey was surrounded by a crowd of disciples and other learners who listened to him while he walked. That was a common way of teaching.

As Jesus and the crowd passed by him, it is likely that the begger got pushed to the side, thus increasing his sense of alienation. When Bartimaeus spoke up crying for help, the people's reaction was like parents when the kids yell while you are trying to watch the news. "Shut up. I am trying to hear this."

But when Bartimaeus was ready to turn his life over to this man, no one was going to stop him. Bartimaeus had one chance. Jesus would pass his way only once. He threw off his cloak to be able to move more quickly.

Last Saturday when our five-year-old son Charlie fell and cut his face badly, I was on a ladder at the highest part of our house and Elise was inside doing housework, dressed in a nightshirt. We both heard the scream and saw a face covered with blood. When you hear your child scream and you see the blood, you do not say, "Let me finish pounding in this nail," or "Let me get on some makeup and a dress." You drop everything. You run. There is nothing more important.

When you know there is a life crisis, you do not say, "One more drink, and I'll get this thing under control." "One last fling, then I'll be faithful." or "Let me just walk over one more person, and I'll be where I want to be in this company and I'll stop treating people this way." The longer we accept our excuses, the harder it becomes, because we have neutralized the sense of crisis.

That blind man did not call on God; he called on Jesus, the son of David. That is the title of one who would come as conquering Messiah, who would return Israel to her national greatness. It does not mean that Bartimaeus knew anything about Jesus' personal ancestry. It was simply one of the names which was natural to refer to the person who was destined to restore the fortunes of Israel.

The followers who were going with Jesus to Jerusalem for the Passover may have created the air of expectancy that suggested this title to Bartimaeus. There is the prophecy in Isaiah 61, one well-known among the Hebrew people, which talked about the coming Messiah and promised he would bring "recovery of sight to the blind."

To call Jesus "son of David" is not an adequate understanding of him. There is no evidence that Bartimaeus understood that it was the Son of God on whom he called. It was not necessary for him to have exactly the correct christological title.

What Jesus accepted was not the title, but the faith to turn his life over. What made him well was trusting in a power to heal him that was higher than his own power. In that one instant he turned his life over to the higher power of Christ, and his life was forever changed. This is the way it works.

Why did the disciples act with such hesitation? By this time in Jesus' ministry, the disciples had been with him for two or three years. They had heard his teachings. They had seen his healings. You would think they would be the ones to take the risk. They should have been the ones who would run up to the blind man and shout, "Your savior is here."

They edged in and out of faith. Those close to the action were not close to understanding. They were trying to conform Jesus to their expectations instead of letting Christ transform them. They were slow in handing themselves over.

A faith commitment is not like deciding what color to paint the family room. You can bring home some color charts and see how it matches the carpets and the couch. You might take a halfway measure and just buy a small can of paint. Paint a section behind the couch. If you don't like it, just move the couch in front of it until you get the color you like. And even if you paint the whole room a color you do not like, you can paint it over.

Turning your life over to a higher power is not like turning your car from regular gas to premium — it costs more, but maybe it will run a little smoother. Sometimes folks try to do that with their faith. We'll try God out a little here for a while, then a little there, then a little somewhere else. When we think our faith is costing too much time and money and freedom, we can treat it like a car that costs too much to run. We trade it in for an economy model faith.

The beggar's life did not just run a little more smoothly. It was transformed. There has to come a leap of faith. There has to come a time when, like the beggar, you truly cannot see a thing, when the best you can manage is the sound of people passing and their voices.

One person who comes to mind is Millard Fuller. Millard Fuller was a graduate of Georgia Tech who made himself very rich very quickly. But he was unsatisfied with his life. Something was missing, but, unlike the blind man, he could not name it specifically. Then he came under the influence of a preacher by the name of Larry Durgin who helped Millard and his wife sort out what his faith was leading him toward.

Fuller, along with his wife, decided to take a huge leap of faith. They gave away all the money they had and started Habitat for Humanity. He gave everything away and now often has former President Jimmy Carter working with Habitat for Humanity.

When life is in crisis, it is important to understand the crisis from the perspective of faith. Crises come to everyone. We think our job is to manage the crisis. "I am unsatisfied with my job. I do not want to do it any more. I will quit and find the job I can manage."

We call on every reserve of strength we have. And sometimes we pull ourselves up by the boot straps out of the trouble, until trouble comes again. A crisis is a gift from God that gives us opportunity to turn whatever is messing up our life over to God.

Bartimaeus had a lifelong crisis. The common wisdom then was you deal with it by begging. But the passing of Christ near his life gave Bartimaeus a chance to make a new choice. He then took a leap of faith, turning to Christ. His response after his life was changed and he was healed, was gratitude. And out of his gratitude came his loyalty in following Jesus.

In the church we ask for people's loyalty, and sometimes the loyalty is hesitant or partial or passing. What is needed first is to take the leap of faith, to let a power greater than ourselves work in us. Then comes the giving out of gratitude.

This story helps me see how specifically we can ask God for help. Maybe there is a neighbor you hate. That hate is making your life unmanageable, and you just cannot do anything about the hatred. Maybe there is a particular thing you want to stop and cannot. Maybe when you get behind the wheel you drive to endanger yourself, your family, and anyone else on the road.

Bartimaeus did not ask Jesus for a general overhaul. He asked to have his eyes healed. We can turn over to God the specific things that trouble us, like hatred for a neighbor or the way we drive. In turning that one thing over to God, everything in his life changed.

The first step has to come first, the step of being honest, of admitting where and how our lives have become unmanageable. Isaiah said this was true for the nation. Bartimaeus said it was true for his life. Now we hear Paul, the great missionary in the history of the church, the author of much of the New Testament, who had a "thorn in the flesh," a debilitating weakness, that made his life unmanageable. If anyone earned God's favor, it was Paul.

He prayed to God to remove it. Nothing doing. So he accepted the power to be able to live with it. "God's power," he assures us, "is made perfect in weakness."

It is only when the clay is made weak, when it is wet, that a sculptor can form it. So it is with our lives. When we are weak, when we are open to God, when we are coachable, when we are teachable, then that power higher than our own can reshape our lives.

What we know is that God's power and grace are revealed through many means. Isaiah saw God's power through the menial task of drawing water. It evoked for him an understanding of the sacramental nature of water. God's power was revealed when a blind man experienced a medical cure. God's power was revealed for Paul when his ailment was not cured, but he was given strength to accept his ailment.

It is a step that believes there is reason for hope. When nations find themselves oppressed, as they did when Isaiah spoke, the inclination is to call on the military to solve the problem. When folks are disabled like Bartimaeus, the inclination is to call for people's pity. When folks have a chronic ailment as did Paul, the inclination is to yield to despair.

It takes courage to "accept the things we cannot change, the courage to change the things we can, and the wisdom to know the difference." That leap of faith is what brings sanity and wholeness.

STEP THREE — FAITH

Isaiah 55:6-9
Hebrews 11:1-7
Matthew 8:5-13

Step three: Made a decision to turn our will and our lives over to God as we understood him.

In seminary I was preparing to take the final exam for my course in Theology 101. In any survey course there is always far more to study than is possible to cover. I tried to study the entire field of theological thought. I reviewed all my class notes. I even resorted to prayer. But neither the study nor the prayer prepared me for the only question on that final exam. The question went something like this:

A man was having trouble in his life and wanted strength to face it. But he found it impossible to pray to a God whom he could not see, so he asked a friend what to do. The friend advised him that if he could not envision an all powerful though invisible God, he should picture in his mind the most powerful thing he could think of.

The man gave it a lot of thought, and the most powerful thing he could imagine was a Greyhound bus. So he knelt down and prayed to this Greyhound bus. And behold, he found insight and help for his trouble by praying to a Greyhound bus. We were then supposed to make comments on the theological propriety of this. I remember saying something to the effect that if it works it is a good start. And I remember passing the final.

Having trouble understanding the existence and nature of God is not unusual. Honestly examining the nature of God and exploring new possibilities as to what this God may truly be like is an eternal human challenge.

When I hear folks say they do not believe in God, I have to ask, "Which God? In which God do you not believe?" We can easily confuse our thoughts about God with the reality of God. We can easily confuse our anger, which seeks vengeance without mercy, with the anger of our God, who may seek vengeance but is always merciful. When we have been wronged, we want restitution. When God is wronged, he seeks reconcilliation. Our God is a God of forgiveness who welcomes us back when we turn to him.

Like the man who prayed to the Greyhound bus, we have all asked questions of God and wondered why God does not answer. It occurs to me that maybe God does not want to answer the particular question we ask. We have a little neighbor boy who is always asking questions. He always wants to know where my boys are and why and what for, and are they being punished and what for, and when are they going to come out to play.

At first I tried to answer his questions. Then I told him that he did not need to know. Then I told him it was none of his business. Now when he asks questions, I just tell him I will tell him what he needs to know, but I will not answer any of his questions. Maybe we ask God questions that God does not choose to answer. Maybe we ask the wrong questions or seek the wrong things.

We seek evidence of things unseen. There is evidence: the birds are fed, the flowers are clothed, the rain falls on the just and the unjust, the sun rises and sets. But that does not meet the criteria we establish. Our thoughts are our thoughts. God's thoughts are God's. And there is a great chasm between them.

Yet we still seek that power that is so much greater than our own. How can we seek God? How can we know God? The psalmist said, "Be still and know that I am God." We cannot shout God down. God does not shout us down. There are verbal skills in speech. There are listening skills as others speak to us. Then there is the skill of listening to the silence. This is the basic skill needed in prayer.

If God's ways are higher than our ways and God's thoughts higher than our thoughts, how can we ever hope to hear what God says? We can, because, even though God is infinitely higher, God is not removed. We are created in God's image. The Bible always talks about God in terms and concepts related to humankind. We think. God thinks. We act. God acts. God is greater than us, but related.

God lets us experience the power, the forgiveness, the love of God in human experience. Earlier this year a group from the church gathered to discuss losses we have experienced. There were a variety of losses we shared with one another, losses by death, loss of health, loss of employment, losses that come through moving.

We found there were common threads in how those various losses were experienced and a common thread in how that loss was managed or was not managed. People's inability to face loss had to do with keeping the loss to themselves, and trying to cope using their own strength. People's ability to cope came with the willingness to share the loss, the pain and the struggle with others, to gain strength from outside themselves.

The willingness to rely on the strength of others and to let others rely on our strength lets us begin to understand and experience relying on God's strength. Our culture values self-sufficiency and celebrates the self-made person. These are the very values that can lead us to rely more on the power of a Greyhound bus than the power of God.

There is a story about a college woman who was having lunch with five other friends. When she silently bowed her head to say grace, the others laughed. Following her silent prayer, she asked the others, "What are you laughing at?" They said, "Well . . . you know," and continued snickering.

"Aren't you grateful?" she asked. "For what? We paid for the food." "But where did you get the money?" she continued. "Family," they said. "Where did they get it?" "Worked for it" was the reply. "But where did they get the strength — where does it all begin?" That evening at supper two of her friends began saying grace. The next day all five of them said it with her.

This God may be high and lifted up, but it is the same God who stoops to offer mercy and abundant pardon for those who are willing to seek and call upon God. Those who live in the illusion of their own strength remove themselves from God.

There is a story told about a man named Sven who was an immigrant from Sweden. Sven had to find work in his new country and landed a jop painting stripes down the center of the highways. This was before there were machines to do this job.

Sven went to work his first day and ended up painting two miles of an almost perfectly straight line down the center of the highway. Sven's boss was never so pleased, for no one had ever before painted two miles of center stripe in one day. The next day out, Sven painted one mile of center stripe, which was still quite good, and his boss was well satisfied.

But the next day Sven only painted half a mile of stripe, and the fourth day he painted just a quarter mile. Finally the boss decided he would have a talk with Sven because he was no longer satisfied with his work. The boss said to Sven, "Sven, you painted two miles on your first day and now you're down to a quarter mile. What's happened?" Sven answered, "Vell, you see each day my bucket get furder and furder away."

Those who seek the Lord often complain that God is getting further and further away. But is it God who has moved away from us, or are we moving away from God?

It takes faith to seek and to turn your life over to God. It is that faith which the writer of Hebrews addresses.

There are some understandings of faith that are inadequate. For some, faith gets conceived of in terms of what is rational versus what is irrational. If it is not rational, then it must be a matter of faith. If it is rational, it is not a matter of faith.

For others, faith means believing something to be true where the evidence is not sufficient to establish knowledge. I read a story about a pastor who called at a home to arrange the funeral of an elderly man who was not a church member nor a professing Christian, but was highly regarded in his community. The widow said, "He was a believer. He believed in God."

Later this pastor speculated, what if, in the early years of their marriage, the wife had asked, "Do you believe in me?" Suppose he answered, "Yes, dear, I believe you exist." The common thinking is that faith progresses to knowledge. It is just the other way. The progression should be from knowledge to faith. "I know you exist. Now I believe in you."

In this marvelous passage, the author of Hebrews describes faith. This is not a definition of faith but a testimony to how that faith works. And the author illustrates this faith in biblical history. As the *New English Bible* translates it, "Faith gives substance to our hope." This is the confidence of those who live in the certainty that God's redemptive work and its future fulfillment are more significant than a particular moment in time.

This spring I planted a garden. It was not long after it was planted that my wife asked me what was planted in each row. I was not sure, because when I planted the seeds, I had the assistance of my two little boys, who kept grabbing packets of seeds to help. Because I was so busy keeping them from helping and retrieving the seed packages, I did not write down what got planted where. In addition, I could not tell which seeds they had scattered in which rows.

There was only one way to know what was planted where. Wait until the plant begins to grow and bear fruit. After a time you can tell the difference between carrots and radishes, between leaf lettuce and romaine, between zucchini and cucumbers. You tell by the fruits the plants bear.

Assurance, hope, faith — these are not based on some naive trust. Time and again God's spirit has borne fruit when all we saw for some time was barren ground. We can not see into the future, let alone far into this day. How can we have faith in where God is leading us? We can look back and know what God has done, the fruit borne by the faithful, the faith of our parents, and from this evidence trust God with this day and tomorrow.

What do you need to make a decision to turn your will and life over to God? Call it faith, call it trust, call it willingness. No more, no less. There is a story of an American tourist who paid a visit to the renowned Polish rabbi Hofetz Chaim. The tourist was astonished to see that the rabbi's home was but a simple, single room. Beside many books, the only furnishings were a table and bench.

"Rabbi," asked the American, "where is all your furniture?" To which Chaim replied, "And where is yours?" "Mine?" asked the tourist with a puzzled tone. "I'm just a visitor here. I'm only passing through." "So am I," answered the rabbi, "So am I." Faith is all we need to pass through this life.

This is not the hope which looks forward with wistful longing. It is the hope which looks forward with utter certainty. It is not the hope which takes refuge in a perhaps. It is the hope which is founded on a conviction.

In seminary I took a course whose very title fascinated me: "The Christian Understanding of History." I will save you three years of seminary education and tell you in one sentence what this was all about.

Our God is made known in the events of history. The writer of Hebrews recounts where God has been made known. He begins with the evidence from creation. "By faith we understand that the world was created by the word of God, so that what is seen was made out of things which do not appear."

The passage we heard read through the chapter and into the next tells of characters in biblical lore from Abel in the book of Genesis on through Scripture. It talks about those who made a faith decision to turn their will and lives over to God.

God's ways are higher than ours. God's thoughts are higher than ours. Yet ours is a God who is present and accessible, even in our ignorance. Helen Keller, when communication had been made by touch of hand through long and patient love, when she could learn about God in Christ, replied in newly-learned language that she knew all this before, but did not know God's name. She had experienced the higher power before, but now knew what to call that power.

We know because we can look at what our God has done in the past and have the assurance of things hoped for, the conviction of things unseen. We do not have to call on the power of a Greyhound bus or any other human creation. We have heard proclaimed this power as the God made known to us in Jesus Christ.

It is as we hear in the verse from "Amazing Grace." "Through many dangers, toils and snares, I have already come; 'Tis grace has brought me safe thus far, and grace will lead me home."

STEP FOUR — COURAGE

Psalm 139:1-6
Acts 9:1-9
Matthew 26:69-75

Step four: Made a searching and fearless moral inventory of ourselves.

The psalmist talks of the God before whom such a searching and fearless moral inventory is both possible and necessary. Ours is a God who, in traditional language, is omniscience and omnipresent, a God who knows all and is everywhere. This Psalm is sometimes called the Psalm of the unavoidable God.

We believe that before our God there are no secret thoughts or actions. All is known by our God. I remember hearing a lecture one time where the speaker had a fantasy. He was going to go into one of those high rise apartment buildings where there is a large panel of buttons to call each apartment. He was going to push all of them at once, say "All is known," then step outside to see how many people jump.

What would you feel like doing if all was known? We have a rule with our boys: If you tell the truth you do not get spanked. If you lie, you do get spanked. We usually need to ask twice. That is because our first response is to defend ourselves. "No I did not do that . . . Okay, I did."

What does it take to get to the point where you can say what the psalmist says? The key word is fearless. The fear of God is the beginning of wisdom, but it is not the end. We have not been given the spirit of fear, as St. Paul tells us, but the spirit of sonship/daughtership. Talking with God about our worst self is okay because God is not going to spank us for telling him what he already knows.

We have to know our God is a God of grace, or else we could not live. Ours is a God who knows all about us, forgives all about us and loves us regardless.

A mentor of mine talked about his feelings when he got married. He said that he thought his wife would love him and stay with him until she found out what he was really like, then it would be all over. She could not know what he was really like and still love him. He found quite the opposite. The more they got to know each other, the more open and honest they were with each other, the more they loved each other.

That, he said, is the miracle of Christian love. In Christian love, our goal is not to hide things from one another. In Christian love we are not supposed to go through life carrying the terrible burden for what we have done or said or thought.

The New Testament reading and the gospel reading tell about two whom God searched and knew. Peter and Paul are the two most significant figures in the early church. They are two men who had some terrible thing they wanted to hide, who made a searching and fearless moral inventory of themselves.

The New Testament reading is the story of Paul's conversion on the Damascus road. Before his conversion Paul was called Saul. (To eliminate confusion I will call him Paul even though this happened when he was Saul.)

Paul was out to persecute followers of "The Way," a name used in the early days to refer to Christians. Paul was not looking for a "way." He was looking for an answer, something specific, something he found in the prescriptions of the law. It is like folks who would rather have "arrived" than face the struggle of being in the process of what life brings.

It reminds me of the time last June when we bought a swing set. Stores do not let you look at the directions until after you have bought the item. The directions began by explaining that it takes experienced workers an hour and 40 minutes to get this swing set assembled, so it might take me a little longer than that.

It took a long time, but it is done and we can just sit back and watch the kids swing. One of the inherent dangers of doing a series on a 12-step process is that it can seem too much like putting together a swing set. Finish the 12th step and you are done.

Swing sets work that way. Matters of faith do not. Last month I listened to a chaplain lead a group of patients who were hospitalized in an addiction recovery center. Someone asked, "At the end of a month here, what step should we be on?"

The chaplain, who is experienced in these 12 steps, said that, if, after a month of intensive work, you had a firm grasp on step one — admitting your life is unmanageable — you are doing very well.

Unlike a product assembly, where you work from step one to 12 and are finished, in this process you return again and again to the basic steps, the basic human struggle of admitting our weakness and turning our life — again and again — over to God. This is not a set of directions and rules and regulations. It is a way of life.

That was not what Paul thought he was looking for. Earlier, Paul had seen the stoning of Stephen, the first Christian martyr. Paul held the cloaks of those who killed him. He had seen the persistence and faith of other Christians. He had witnessed the shedding of blood.

I think here of people who join the Ku Klux Klan. This group is sure it has the answer: Espouse the cause of white superiority; hate blacks and Jews. Those rules are clear and easy to follow. They put on the robe and join the cross burning. But something happens.

Maybe they see firsthand what happens when racial hatred runs out of control, as it did in Forsythe County. Maybe they have a child bring home a new friend of a different race or religion or culture. As they watch the children play together, something breaks through the hatred and they hear a voice saying, "Why are you so filled with hate when it is so much better to be filled with love?

Paul was not setting out to do a moral inventory of himself. He was out to destroy the followers of the Way. Paul must have been certain that he was doing good. After all, he was defending what he believed to be the true faith. As often happens with "true believers," the intensity of his effort was his way of convincing himself of his doubts.

He was not just content with driving Christians from Jerusalem. Because they were being severely persecuted, the church in Jerusalem had been forced underground, and refugees were reported to have reached Damascus. They must be pursued and rooted out wherever they fled, not only within the frontiers of the land of Israel, but beyond them as well.

It is about 140 miles from Jerusalem to Damascus. The journey would be made on foot and would take about a week. Paul's only companions were the officers of the Sanhedrin, a kind of police force. But because he was a Pharisee, he could have nothing to do with them. So he walked alone, alone with his thoughts.

Just before Damascus the road climbs Mount Hermon, and down below lay Damascus. That region has one characteristical meteorological phenomenon. When the hot air of the plain meets the cold air of the mountain range, violent electrical storms result. Just at that moment there came a blinding light and out of the storm and in it Christ spoke to Paul.

There are various and sundry speculations as to what happened to Paul on that road. It may well have been the intensity of the thunderstorm that made him listen to God in a whole new way. Others say it was hysterical blindness. Paul did dictate his letters instead of write them himself, and when he did write, he wrote in large print. Others think Paul had epilepsy. This might tie in with Paul's later reference to his "thorn in the flesh."

Paul's conversion reminds me a bit of the courtroom scene from every Perry Mason show. The innocent party has been charged with guilt. The guilty party is on the stand or in the courtroom watching the trial. The evidence builds and builds. There is that one last piece of evidence detective Paul Drake brings in, and in an instant the plea of innocence becomes an admission of guilt.

Paul had been fighting and fighting and fighting against the Way of Christ, but as he dealt with the saints, the evidence continued to mount against what he was doing with his life. The last piece of evidence came in, and then the surrender. He who had intended to enter Damascus with an avenging fury was led by the hand, blind and helpless.

For three days — a holy number — he fasted, a penitent fast. And he said nothing. He needed to get things right with God, but what was he to say? He realized that God knew all. How could he ask forgiveness?

Whatever happened on the road, God did something to him. His life was transformed. He stopped fighting the Way of Christ and started following the Way of Christ. He changed from chief persecutor to chief missionary.

This is the story of Paul's conversion. The word conversion literally means having your life turn around. I have talked with people whose lives have gone through a substantial change. They can point to the hinge experience of their life. But when I refer to that as their conversion, the reaction is often that I did not understand what they were explaining. This was not, I am sometimes told, a religious experience. Their entire life changed, but they did not see God in charge.

Paul could have done that. He could have analyzed what happened. "I guess I have a phobia with lightning and I lost my senses." "It is just hysterical blindness." "It was just exhaustion. The trip wore me out." "I have been under too much stress." No. What happened was God spoke to him and he listened and he let God forgive him and he let God change his life.

This brings us to the story of Peter. Some days before Peter had promised Jesus, "Even if I must die with you, I will not deny you (Matthew 26:35)." But things happened. There was conflict at the last supper; then there was the arrest in the Garden of Gethsemene where Peter and the others fled.

When Jesus was inside the house of Caiaphas, the high priest, being questioned, Peter showed a lot of courage in even going into that courtyard, and then sticking around after he has been twice identified.

He wanted to be brave, but he was like a child caught in a lie. "I didn't do it." Then one lie leads to another. Aristotle said that the penalty for telling a lie is that the liar is not believed when he tells the truth.

We want to hide our lies and ourselves from that God who judges us. I talked with a teenager who told me that when she was a pre-teen she tried to kill her mother. Fortunately she did not succeed. But after that when she went to church she would hide under the pews. That was her response to her guilt, to try to hide from God.

Peter's response to his guilt was healthy. He stopped the lies. He did not try to hide his guilt. He cried. Blessed are those who mourn, for they shall be comforted. Blessed are those who mourn when they look at their lives, for they shall be comforted.

At about the same time both Peter and Judas betrayed Jesus, each in his own way. The difference in their betrayal is a matter of degree, just as each of us to some degree betrays our calling. But the difference in how Judas and Peter responded to their awareness of what they had done wrong, was not a difference of degree, but difference of kind.

Both men did wrong. Both men became painfully aware they had done wrong. You recall Judas throwing the money back at those who gave it to him. God knew what Peter and Judas did. God did not destroy either of them. But Judas destroyed himself. Peter wept but returned.

Let us conclude with two observations. Ours is a God who searches and knows us. Christ knew Peter would fail. He told him so. God knew how Peter had persecuted the Christians. Our God knows our weakness before we even do the wrong. Our God loves us, from the greatest to the least, and knowing us, loves us. How else could these two who had done such wrong come back and operate with such power? The God who sees us as we truly are loves us as we truly are.

Second observation. How did the church get these stories of Peter and Paul? Peter and Paul must have told these stories themselves. If I had done what they had done — so overtly denied Jesus, so openly persecuted the followers of Jesus — and tried to cover it up we would have "Christgate."

If the early church was into cover-ups, this would be the event to hide. But it was not hidden, because Peter and Paul were willing to tell their story.

Paul's driving ambition was to strike fear in the hearts of Christians. As a Christian himself he was fearless before any such threats. The same Peter who was fearful of the question of a servant girl was touched by the grace of God, so that a short time later he would be fearless in the presence of the mob on Pentecost. It was not because Peter or Paul were terribly virtuous, but simply because of the great love of our God who empowers those with the courage to honestly place our whole lives in God's care.

STEP FIVE — INTEGRITY

Isaiah 6:1-8
1 John 1:5-10
John 4:16-24

Step five: Admitted to God, to ourselves, and to another human being, the exact nature of our wrongs.

I have been accused during this sermon series of being too sober — in my preaching. So: joke de jour. A minister, a priest and a rabbi were having lunch one day. They were talking about the spiritual support they gave the members of their congregation: listening to their confessions, saying words of absolution, visiting them when they were ill and comforting them in times of loss.

What the minister, priest and rabbi found they had in common was the sense of having ministered to their congregation, but having no one to minister to them. So they decided to go together for a retreat and provide one another with care.

They gathered on the appointed day and decided that they would begin with confession and absolution. The minister said that since Jews had been atoning for their sins for thousands of years, the rabbi should go first.

The rabbi said, "You know, I love my wife and would never cheat on her, but sometimes in a crowd where no one can tell who did it, I just cannot resist giving the ladies a little pinch." The minister and the priest assured the rabbi that God loves him and forgives him, and that they love him and forgive him.

Then the minister suggested that the priest go next, because for hundreds of years Catholics have practiced confession. The priest said, "You know I have taken a vow of poverty, but there are days when it is so hard to live on my little stipend. And there are times when I look at all the money we make on bingo, and I just can't help taking just a little of it for myself just to pay the bills.'' The rabbi and the minister assured the priest that God loves him and forgives him, and that they love him and forgive him.

Then it was the minister's turn. He said, ''I know that God loves me and forgives me, but I don't think you will feel that way when I tell you about my besetting sin.'' The priest and the rabbi sought to comfort him and asked, ''What awful sin have you committed?'' He said, ''I'm a terrible gossip!''

The Old Testament text tells about the struggle some 2,700 years ago of the prophet Isaiah as he faced the nature of his wrong. It happened the year the Uzziah, king of Israel, died. Uzziah was the greatest king of Israel since Solomon ruled hundreds of years before. Now he was gone, the nation's throne was empty and the nation's future was unsure.

This is the story of Isaiah's confession and his calling, not Isaiah's theory about guilt, forgiveness and calling, his personal experience. ''I saw the Lord.'' When Isaiah had this overwhelming experience of God's presence, he also had an overwhelming sense of being unclean.

The temple area in which Isaiah had his vision was about 30 feet square and 30 feet high. I mention that because in our church we need to know that the size of the revelation of God has nothing to do with the size of the place of worship. What matters is not the size of the building but the size of the vision.

There is that tendency to judge ourselves in comparison to other people. If I compare myself to others, I will come out as well or poorly as my ego allows. I am fatter or thinner, earn more or less, gossip more or less, play a better game of tennis or worse. It is the ultimate comparison with God that brought Isaiah the true evaluation of himself. Confession before God is the necessary starting point, because God's holiness is the standard by which we are judged.

In comparison to God, Isaiah understood his uncleanness. It was not just his problem. It is a dirty world out there. We do not invent temptation and sin. It is waiting for us. We are unclean people in the midst of an unclean world.

Confession is not any more fun than having an appendectomy is fun. It is not a recreational activity. It is necessary surgery. We are led to confession because of what is on the other side.

One of the slogans popular today is, "Just say 'No.'" For some people that is all it takes. They say "No" to drugs and they are fine. But a lot of folks can see no reason to say "No." They will tell you, "I like what drugs do to me." Or they will say, "Everybody does it." Isaiah first had to say, "I am unclean." Then he had to say my world, my peers, are unclean. "Everybody does it" does not give anything moral approval.

In the church there are two basic kinds of confession: general confession and personal confession. That is because we need to do both kinds of confession. To confess the exact nature of our wrongs — I kicked my dog yesterday — we run the risk of ignoring the weightier nature of our sin — I never kicked my neighbor, but I hate him. To confess only the general nature of our wrong — I hate my neighbor — we can avoid the specifics — and I drove over his trash can with my truck. We need to do both — general confession as we do every Sunday, and the personal confession.

As a Protestant I grew up being told that we do not have to be like those Catholics. We do not have to go to a priest to confess our sins. That is true. You do not have to come to me to confess your sins. Isaiah does not tell us about anyone else being present when he confessed his uncleanness to God. Some Catholics and former Catholics will tell you what a turn-off the confessional can be. But some will also tell you how much it has helped them with life's journey. Having a confessor is good for our spiritual and emotional health.

What is important, whether we primarily follow the route of general confession or private confession, is to be led to the point Isaiah reached: to honestly see ourselves and our world for what we are.

The First Letter of John is more biblical foundation in understanding that this message is for all of us, not simply a message for the drunk lying in the gutter or the criminal in jail.

Our capacity to have fellowship with one another has to do with our capacity for confession. "If we say we have no sin we deceive ourselves."

It reminds me of the story of a family arriving late for the service at a new church. They came in as the congregation was repeating, "We have done those things which we ought not to have done and we have left undone those things which we ought to have done." The wife turns to the husband and says, "I think we finally found a church where we fit in."

There are folks who choose to deceive themselves. You may have heard the little verse which goes like this:

> At three I had a feeling of
> Ambivalence toward my brothers,
> And so it follows naturally,
> I poisoned all my lovers.
> But now I'm happy, I have learned
> The lesson this has taught;
> That everything I do that's wrong
> Is someone else's fault.

Living in the midst of people of unclean lips, it is easy to find someone else being at fault for whatever is wrong in our lives. We admitted to God, to ourselves and to another human being, the exact nature of everyone else's wrongs.

Our God is a God who is not content to leave us in the dark. There is a story told of a boy from the country who visited relatives in London for the first time. This was in the days when London had streetlights, but they were unknown in the country. That first night in London the boy sat on the front porch of the house and gazed in amazement at the wondrous sights of the city.

As he looked down the street, he saw a man making his way toward him. The man would stop at each corner and pause beside the lamp post, and then a round globe of light would burst forth through the darkness as the man lit the lamp.

As the boy watched in wonderment, the street gradually changed from darkness to a place of light. He became so excited that he ran into the house and exclaimed, "There's a man outside poking holes in the darkness." Ours is a God who pokes holes in the darkness — if we confess our sins he is faithful and just.

I read somewhere a comment by H. L. Mencken to the effect that conscience is what makes us think somebody might be watching. It makes a difference to know that our God is watching us.

The text from this letter of St. John also makes clear that true faith produces both fellowship with God and fellowship with one another. They are inseparable. We need the integrity of being honest to God and one another. One reason we need to confess to another is that God works through others. We come to know we are forgiven by God when we experience forgiveness through others.

This is the sacramental statement. "If we walk in the light as he is in the light, we have fellowship with one another, and the blood of Jesus cleanses us from all sin." Isaiah had that mystical experience of cleansing expressed in poetic terms. Here we find it in new covenant terms, cleansing through the blood of Christ.

Another biblical resource for honestly facing our life is the story of Jesus confronting a woman about her particular sin. This was not a general issue. Jesus was dealing with the exact nature of wrong in this woman's life.

There is no clue in the text how Jesus knew about the woman's personal life. He just knew and confronted her on it. Did you notice how she tried to shift the conversation? When Jesus unexpectedly reveals his insight into her personal life, she immediately tried to shift the conversation by talking about religion, the differences between Jews and Samaritans.

Jesus reminded her that authentic worship has to do with the truth. It was her willingness to be honest about her life that led this woman to know who Christ was.

Hans-Ruedi Weber relates a story from East Africa. A simple woman always walked around with her bulky Bible. She was never parted from it. So the villagers began to tease her.

45

"Why always the Bible?" they asked. "There are so many other books you could read."

Yet the woman kept on living with her Bible, neither disturbed nor angered by all the teasing. But finally one day, she knelt down in the midst of those who laughed at her. She held up the Bible, high above her head, and she said with a great smile, "Yes, of course there are many books which I could read. Yet there is only one book which reads me."

God called Isaiah to face the uncleanness of himself and his world. Jesus called the woman of Samaria to be truthful about her past. St. John called us not to deceive ourselves in thinking we have no sin.

God's intention is never for us to live in eternal regret for the words that have come from our lips, as Isaiah could have. God's intention is never for us to live with eternal embarrassment for our past life, as the woman of Samaria could have. God's intention is never for us to live with an eternal cloud over our fellowship with one another.

We are called to honestly admit to God, ourselves and another the exact nature of our wrongs so, like Isaiah, we can hear God's calling to a greater life; like the woman, we can be freed of past guilt and be able to worship God rightly; and like the early church, we can have fellowship with one another with all the fullness and richness possible for those who love Christ and follow him.

STEP SIX — WILLINGNESS

Isaiah 1:12-20
Hebrews 4:14-16
John 5:2-9a

Step six: Were entirely ready to have God remove all these defects of character.

Here is Isaiah, whom we saw in last week's text being so awed by God's presence, so totally aware of his uncleanness before God. His was a majestic experience of worship. In this morning's text God speaks through Isaiah, questioning the validity of the people's worship.

The local Chamber of Commerce recently came out with a listing of the best of Gwinnett. It listed the best pizza, the best athlete, the best country road. And it listed the best sermon. I do not know how many of the members of this congregation were involved in that vote. I just know I did not win.

Aside from that offense, I found that whole notion of voting for the best sermon an extremely inappropriate measure of the life of a Christian church. Isaiah looked at all of the ways by which worship was judged, and said that the things that get you listed as "Best in the County" are not what God is looking at.

Worship and preaching and singing are not intended to please people, but to glorify God. How can we measure the quality of worship? How can we determine the quality of our confession? Isaiah makes it plain. "Cease to do evil, learn to do good; seek justice, correct oppression; defend the fearless, plead for the widow."

This is the litmus test to measure our worship and life together. Where have we turned our own lives and our world from evil to good?

In preparation for the upcoming religious leaders' conference on adolescents and addiction which I am hosting, I visited the denominational book stores in Atlanta. I visited what is probably the largest denominational book store in Atlanta to find out what books, church school curriculum and/or youth program materials they had on adolescents and drug and alcohol abuse.

After an extensive search of their store and catalogues, they discovered they had absolutely nothing on the subject. While I was waiting, a man came in and asked for material on "childhood salvation." They had a whole section of material on childhood salvation. I stood there in amazement.

What are you saving kids from if you are not saving them from drugs? To attend your solemn assemblies? Or are you saving them to learn to do good, seek justice, correct oppression, defend the fatherless, plead for the widow?

There are many forms of worship, many kinds of solemn assemblies, but there is only one true end of worship. Isaiah's worship experience ended with the statement, "Here am I. Send me." True worship has to do with both confession of our faults and being willing then to act for God.

Some churches will say in their bulletin, "Enter to worship, depart to service." Others say, "Service begins when the worship is ended." The worship and praise of God are only the beginning, the energy charge, the course correction which send us out to change what is wrong in our lives and our world.

I learned something this week about the importance of integrating our words of faith and action. I learned this past week about the fascination of many adolescents with Satanism. It is a common theme with some musical groups. Some adolescents wear jewelry and/or clothes with Satanic symbols. I discovered that a major appeal of Satanism for many youth is as a way of rejecting the church, rejecting the religious establishment of their parents just as God did through Isaiah.

It is a rejection of the scarlet sins of the church. Our best weapon against the appeal of evil represented in Satanism is to cleanse ourselves, as Isaiah calls us to do.

The author of Hebrews gives us the promise that we are not doing that by our own power alone. There are a lot of folks who will come to church as long as all is well in their lives, as long as there are none of those scarlet sins to which Isaiah refers. But make one big mistake, one nasty sin, and they just do not believe they can ever walk in a church again.

That is tragic. That is like thinking that as long as you are healthy you can visit your friends in the hospital, but if you should become ill, you are forbidden from entering the hospital for your own healing.

It has been appropriately stated that the church is not a museum for saints but a hospital for sinners. We have all done things of which we are not proud. But because of our Savior, we can still come here in confidence that those scarlet sins can be removed.

When you have a big problem you like to have someone you can trust there to help you. If your engine is making a funny noise, you want a mechanic you can depend on. This past week I had to replace two tires on my truck. It would have been nice to have a friend I knew I could depend on to sell me the right product at the right price.

The author of Hebrews tells us we have the insider, one who has had all the common experiences — like flat tires — but one who got through life without sin. He is our High Priest. The book of Hebrews refers to the Jewish worship custom of the high priest each year on the Day of Atonement, passing through the outer sanctuary which any priest could enter, on through the curtain beyond it, and into the Holy of Holies itself.

This "passing through" was the great moment of his priesthood, it was the act for which the high priesthood existed. We do not have to wait a year or a day. As we found in last week's story of Jesus and the woman of Samaria, again we find Jesus having particular insight into a person, for he has gone through all we have gone through.

The setting is by the pool of Bethsaida. Beneath the pool was a subterranean stream, and every now and again the stream bubbled up and disturbed the water of the pool. It was believed that an angel of the Lord went down at certain seasons into the pool and troubled the water. People would wait for the moving of the water. Whoever stepped in first after the troubling of the water was healed of whatever disease he had.

There lay on a pallet a man who had been ill for 38 years. The pallet was a light, flexible mat which could be rolled up and carried. It does not mean that the man had been lying at the pool for all 38 years without ever leaving. But he had been ill that long and somehow had never gotten into the healing waters.

In this little story there is a great deal for us. There is a rejection of superstition. That is a comment for anyone who tries to schedule life changes via the horoscope. There is a rejection of the way of life which involves some outside force coming in to take care of my ills.

I think of folks who always put a couple of dollars on a number, always buy a lottery ticket, always lay out too much for the weekend game, and always find themselves losing out. They are looking for something to happen to them to get them out of their situation.

There is in this story the rejection of the neurotic appeal of misery. I read a sermon on this passage in which the preacher spoke of this attitude of enjoying misery: "Tomorrow, maybe; tomorrow maybe I'll pull myself together and try a little harder; but right now leave me alone to grovel in my guilt a little longer; it's so sweet, so sickly sweet. Let me wait a while, until I manage to make it to those miraculous waters they say are so painless to take. Someone will come along to carry me, sooner or later — maybe tomorrow — I hope not today.

I knew a man who worked right up to his 65th birthday and retired. As soon as he retired, he began developing minor ailments. When I and others in the church would visit him, there would only be one conversation: how his ailments were ruining his retirement. Each visit he had the same conversation with me and everyone else.

I found my visits becoming further and further apart, and others told me the same thing. It was always the same conversation. We got tired of it. Finally it occurred to me that this man would rather be alone in his ailments than to be with his friends. Excuses can be good company.

There is a real luxury in feeling sorry for yourself, especially if you can convince yourself and everyone else that you are worthless, that change is hopeless. It cuts down the demands on you. This story is a rejection of blaming our problems on others.

There was a young preacher with an attractive wife who liked new clothes. She spent too much and they were in debt. Finally they had a long talk and she agreed to buy nothing without first talking it over.

Then she went to town and came back with a new dress. The young preacher said to her, "But, my dear, you promised me." She replied, "I know I did, but the devil tempted me." He said, "You should have said, 'Get thee behind me, Satan.' " "Oh," she replied, "I did, and he whispered, 'It fits so beautifully in the back.' "

This story is a rejection of blaming the conditions of the world for my problems. It reminds me of a cartoon I saw where the foreman of the jury stood and said the defendant is not at fault. He is a victim of social deficiency. The jury is guilty and ready to serve time.

This story is a rejection of smothering pity. "Oh, you poor dear. Thirty-eight years and no one said, 'You go first.' or 'Take my hand I'll help you get in.' That is terrible. People are so thoughtless and selfish. I really feel sorry for you. Thirty-eight years. Just think of that."

This story is also a rejection of insensitivity. "Look, it is not my problem, it's not my fault. Your father ought to help you. Go get yourself some welfare." This is not a justification for the hardness of heart.

Some folks think it is always okay to be gruff and insensitive. That is not what the gospel is about. Jesus did not yell, "Look, do you want to be healed or what?" to make the man feel worse about himself. It was a healing question out to remove the obstacle, not to crush a frail ego.

This is a story about Jesus giving the man, not what he asked for, but what he needed. Jesus did not do what the men wanted, because he wanted too little. All he seemed to want was pity. Instead, Jesus gave him what he needed and was too timid to hope for. And it was in the cause of this higher goal that Jesus helped him. Like a loving parent, God sometimes denies what we ask in order to give us something we need.

At the addiction conference this week the main speaker has a simple message. Addiction is a medical problem. Plain and simple. It is medical, it is chemical. What do you do with a medical problem? You go to a doctor. What does the doctor do? The doctor gives you a shot or a pill or performs an operation. That works very well if your problem is an acute appendicitis or diabetes.

But other times the problem is not cured by some external solution. Healing is not always a matter of the right operation or medication. The other part of the conference speaker's point is that while addiction is primarily a medical problem, the only workable, long-term solution is spiritual. That is the only cure for addiction.

The cure for much of what ails us is spiritual. It has to do with our relationship with God. It has to do with letting go and letting God.

This story has to do with putting our life and our healing in proper relationship with God. There is a loving accountability before God. God does not do a random survey of humanity to see who is responsible for my bad habits. There is only one person responsible.

Martin Luther once wrote, "Everyone must fight his own battle with death by himself, alone. We can shout into one another's ears, but everyone must be prepared finally to meet death alone. I will not be with you then, nor you with me. Therefore everyone must know for himself the chief things of Christianity and be armed therewith."

The issue in this text is, do you really want to be healed, do we really want to be changed? Last week we considered the issue of confession, confessing to God, to ourselves and to another human being the exact nature of our wrongs. This is the next and necessary step. It is one thing to say that I know I have been ill for 38 years, but the question is, do you really want to be healed? Or are you, despite what you have said to God, to yourself, to another human being, really content with all in your life?

The issue in the text is cooperation. Is God trying to do something with your life and you do not want it to happen? You may recall that famous painting by Holman Hunt, of Christ standing at the door and knocking. It is based on the text from Revelation 3:20: "Behold, I stand at the door and knock; if anyone hears my voice and opens the door, I will come into him and eat with him, and he with me."

What is so striking about Hunt's painting is that there is no door handle on the outside, only on the inside. Christ knocks on the door, but waits for us to open. Do you want to be healed? If so, let God in to do it.

The question of Christ was not cruel or curious. The question clearly implied that you can be healed. The promise is that we are free from all the scar tissue of yesterday's failures and foolishness. We are free from tomorrow's uncertainties.

The angels of God may trouble the waters that bring healing, but God leaves it to us to act, if we really want to be healed.

STEP SEVEN — HUMILITY

Psalm 51:1-14
2 Timothy 2:20-26
Matthew 23:25-36

Step seven: "Humbly asked Him to remove our shortcomings."

Psalm 51 is basic to the biblical foundation of this step. The introduction to this Psalm sets the context for its writing. Nathan, a prophet of God, went to David, the King of Israel, after David's affair with Bathsheba. David had gained fame and power and wealth. David had not only committed adultery with Bathsheba. When he discovered she was pregnant with his child, David sent her husband, Uriah, into battle, had the troops around him pull back so he would be killed.

David was guilty of lust, intrigue, adultery, treachery and arranging the murder of Uriah. He broke half the ten commandments in one affair. To such serious guilt, this Psalm is addressed.

Nathan then went to David and confronted him with his guilt. There came the awful burst of awareness when David realized what he had done.

David, or whoever actually wrote this about David, was aware that his sin was not simply something involving Bathsheba or her husband or the child conceived out of wedlock. What he did to them was first a sin against God.

When the prodigal son returned home, he said to his father, "I have sinned against heaven and before you." This does not focus first on what moral laws we have broken or what people we have offended, but on the offence to God, the laws of God we have broken.

The psalmist was aware of the inherent weakness we all have. "In sin did my mother conceive me." This is not a moral condemnation of sex, but a commentary on the whole human condition. But even that is no excuse.

His plea talks of ". . . the bones which thou hast broken." It is not clear that he meant this literally, although serious illness can cause us to take a long look at our life. Maybe he was physically ill. But whatever the circumstances, for him it was a time for self-examination. He knew his physical and/or spiritual condition came as a result of God's punishment for his sin.

He sought to reveal the "inward parts," the muck and mire that is at the bottom of the soul of us all so that he might be cleansed.

Three terms are used for his condition. The first is "transgression," which is a sin of conscious rebellion, the act which violates a known standard, like a private slapping a general. The second word is "iniquity," which is the sin of injustice. That is when the boss recommends a 40 percent raise for himself and five percent for those under him. The third word is "sin," which literally means missing an aimed-at mark. That is like promising ourselves, our family and God that we will spend 10 hours a week with our family, but ending up spending only 30 minutes a week.

So the psalmist pleads for cleansing. There are three words he uses for forgiveness. The first is "blot out," which means to wipe off. It is a term used for the ritual act performed by the priest of washing off into the water curses which he had written on a tablet (Numbers 5:23). It means complete removal of a very damaging entry in God's record book.

The second term is "wash," which refers to the method of washing garments by thorough-going treading with the feet. It is a plea for God to bleach away my sin. Remove the stain of my actions.

The third is "declare me clean," which is a ceremonial term used in the ritual in which the priest pronounces the worshiper clean. *The Anchor Bible* translates this in its literal meaning: "Unsin me . . . delete all my crimes (vv. 9a, 11b)."

The Psalm writer strikes a bargain with God. If God will forgive him, if God will help him get out from under the load of guilt, he will feel free to do things for God. It does not end with him just feeling bad about what he had done. The best that secular psychology can do is help remove our sense of guilt. Our faith is what moves us to the joy of sharing the good news.

Whether it is grieving over a death or grieving for deeds of the past, bargaining is part of the grief process. "God, if you will grant me this favor, I will do this for you . . ." The psalmist is in grief over his sin-filled condition. Therefore he bargains, "Help me get rid of this load of guilt and I am going to tell everyone how good it is to know God forgives, how good it is to walk without being stooped over with guilt."

It is the movement from being the mission field to being the missionary. Our awareness of guilt is the beginning. The end is to be part of the triumphal and joyful community of faith.

The letter to Timothy picks up where the Psalm ends. The New Testament lesson was written by Paul to a young missionary, Timothy. The advice he is giving is how to help those being crushed by their sense of guilt to receive and live this good news.

What would I do if I stopped getting angry all the time? What would I do if I stopped lying to people? How would I start to relate in a decent way to the co-worker who causes me to drool? What would I do with my kids if I stopped yelling at them? What comes after my guilt is removed, my sin taken away, and I am grateful to God? How do I show that?

Paul used the analogy of kitchen plates. He spoke like a man who spent little time in the kitchen, which is to say it is not a very good analogy. What he tried to say was this: The great house is the church, and the Christians are the various utensils. Like a kitchen with different utensils, in the church there are all sorts of conditions of persons. Whatever our place on the shelf, it is for us to make ourselves useful to God.

A plate may look beautiful, but up high on the shelf it is of no practical value. Another plate may have a great deal of practical value, but it never gets cleaned up, so it is not used. It is the cleanliness of the inside and what fills the vessel that determines its value.

Paul also gives the advice that for us to succeed in this mission work, there has to be honesty in asking God to give us strength to do what we ought to do, both in our personal life and in our church life. We are bound for failure if we try to depend on our own power.

Avoid being filled with evil by filling yourself with good. Your life will be filled with some spirit, with some activity. Your mind will be filled with some thoughts. We need God's strength to shun youthful passions and instead seek to fill our thoughts and actions with righteousness, faith, love and peace.

We know that in the church, we have not always reached the high calling to which we have been called. Paul talks about a major reason for that failure. I have heard someone define true community as occurring when the last person you want to attend a meeting shows up first, and if they don't, someone else just like them will.

Some think that their job is to purge the community of all errors in thinking. Some think there has to be someone in opposition or something is wrong. I remember my father telling me that in every church there needed to be an "SOB," and my father designated himself to fill that role. I trust that now he is singing with the angels, that he has mellowed.

Contrary to such thinking, what the gospel says is: "Having nothing to do with stupid, senseless controversies; you know that they breed quarrels. And the Lord's servant must not be quarrelsome but kindly to everyone, an apt teacher, forebearing, correcting his opponents with gentleness."

Most arguments reflect our willingness to have God remove someone else's shortcomings. Whether we are right or wrong, most arguments reflect our willingness to have God correct someone else's failures. However good our intentions, Paul has other advice. We do not win people to the way of Christ by winning an argument between us and them.

I believe the style of "invitational evangelism" is more appropriate. We do not club people over the head with the truth, nor badger them into repentance. We wait for God to let the person hear. Since we do not know when God is going to do that, we may freely and frequently invite folks to accept a new way of life, but leave them with the free choice to accept or reject this.

"God may perhaps grant that they will repent and come to know the truth, and they may escape from the snare of the devil, after being captured by him to do his will."

There is an interesting note at the end of this passage. Paul lifted up the promise that "They may escape from the snare of the devil. The Lord may grant them a change of heart and show them the truth, and thus they may come to their senses . . ." The Greek word for change of heart literally means "to become sober again" or "come to one's senses." We have been in the therapy business from the start!

It is to such a new life that we issue the invitation. People may have trouble listening because they are so aware of their sins that they cannot believe that God will really forgive them and give them a new life. Others cannot enter a new life of faith because they may not be willing to admit before God their true nature.

The gospel tells us about Jesus talking to a group of folks like that. The Pharisees were a group of religious people who were certain of their own goodness. The self-pronounced righteous were often in conflict with Christ.

This passage finds Christ talking bluntly. It does not sound like gentle Jesus, meek and mild. It is more like the voice David must have heard when Nathan confronted him with the sins of his passion.

There are seven "woes" with which Christ confronted them. The word translated "woe" is more an expression of sorrow and lamentation than of threat and fury. "You sorry creatures, trapped in your illusions of righteousness. I want you to really see yourself." It is like a doctor pleading with a patient to give up a deadly habit or have a life-saving operation.

The passage we heard had the last three "woes." The cleansing of cups and of hands before eating was an important ceremony with the Jews, not on grounds of hygiene or physical cleanliness, but because of the danger of ceremonial impurity.

Jesus said that if you were as careful to see that the contents of vessels were derived in honorable and just ways, you would not have to worry very much about the ceremonial cleanliness of the outside of the cup. You worry about how to knot your tie and fluff your hair. Better for you to worry about how you earned the money to buy the tie and get your hair done.

The next "woe" had to do with graves. They did not have graveyards laid out as we do. The commonest place for tombs was by the roadside. They considered walking over a grave caused a person to be polluted, and in order to enter the temple this had to be avoided.

At the time Jesus spoke, the roads were crowded with pilgrims traveling to Jerusalem for the Passover. Before the Passover, graves were chalked off and the stones whitewashed so the pilgrims going to the city might not inadvertently walk over them. These tombs would literally have glittered in the sun, having just been whitewashed.

For a person to become unclean on the way to the Passover Feast would be like spilling grape juice all over the new outfit just as you were on the way out the door for an Easter service. We all try to look good going to church. We are sparkling clean. But what about the inside? Are we just like those whitewashed tombs, just full of dead bones inside? Are we like T.S. Eliot's hollow man?

The seventh woe finds Jesus speaking to those who get tied up in the "if only's" of life. "If only I had lived in the brave days of the past, I would not have done the evil that my ancestors did. If only I were there, how much better I would have been than my fathers. They were the ones who killed the special messengers of God. We don't do that." This is the spirit of self-righteousness that Jesus rejects.

They honored those whom their ancestors ignored and sometimes slayed. Abel is the first one killed in the Bible. In the Jewish ordering of the books of the Bible, Zechariah is the last (2 Chronicles 24:20-21). Zechariah was a faithful priest of God who was murdered within the court of the temple when he tried to call the people to obey the commandments of God.

We can honor those messengers by raising memorials to their greatness, like the Lincoln Memorial or the King Center. Christ said that monuments can be a superficial way of showing honor. True honor is shown by living in the spirit of the prophets and carrying into practice their teachings. It is nice to fantasize about how good we would be if we lived in pre-Civil War days when slavery still existed in this state. But living in a past we never knew can cause us to miss the opportunities of the present which is where God is claiming us.

Like much of what appears in the Bible, humility is not popular today. We do not like to hear the woes of our condition. We are taught to admire rugged independence, an upwardly mobile ambition, the ability to stand up for ourselves. Humility brings reminders of feeling bad about ourselves, embarrassing moments that made us feel small, the terribly awkward time at the junior high dance.

Christian humility really has nothing to do with putting down ourselves or being put down by others. Humility has to do with understanding our worth before God. Humility has to do with the reality of our condition and the need for a power higher than our own. That is what the Scripture speaks to in ways people often do not like: the truth about our human condition.

Robert Burns talked about the gift to see ourselves as others see us. What we work on the hardest is for others to see us as we see ourselves.

What we should let God do for us is to help us see ourselves as we really are, not as others see us or as we see ourselves, but to see ourselves as God sees us — all the sins and all the promise of salvation.

That is what these passages of Scripture are about. They help us see where we are on our journey of life and faith, so that in spirit and in truth we will be led to humbly ask God to remove all our shortcomings.

STEP EIGHT — LOVE

Psalm 19:7-13
2 Corinthians 5:16-21
Matthew 7:7-14

Step eight: Made a list of all persons we harmed, and became willing to make amends to them all.

I can see the scene now. They are meeting over a three-martini lunch to plan out the advertising strategy. They struggle with what hook they will use to lure people to their product. One of them says, "Think of this? What revives the soul, makes wise the simple, rejoices the heart, enlightens the eyes, is to be more desired than gold and is sweeter than honey?"

What could be the product? How about a vacation home in the Caribbean? Would it be winning the New York State lottery? Could it be a new miracle, feel-good medicine? Is it the ultimate labor-saving-housework-made-effortless machine? Instead they find out they are on Candid Camera and someone reads the totally unexpected:

> *The law of the Lord is perfect,*
> *reviving the soul;*
> *the testimony of the Lord is sure,*
> *making wise the simple;*
> *the precepts of the Lord are right,*
> *rejoicing the heart;*
> *the commandment of the Lord is pure,*
> *enlightening the eyes;*
> *More to be desired are they than gold . . .*
> *sweeter also than honey.*

You expect the Bible to be in favor of obeying the Law. But what is said about keeping the Law is not expected. What the first part of this psalm says about God is what is expected. It sings praises to the creator of nature. God's revelation in nature for most of us is probably the first dawning awareness of the reality and greatness of God.

But this hymn is also about God as the creator of the Law. The first part of the Psalm has to do with the creation of nature, the second with the Law that is redeeming God's creation. This is the on-going activity of God.

Normally, our first concern about breaking the Law is the possible consequences we might receive for violating civil or criminal laws. Weekdays when I drive to church, I drive through a school zone. There are flashing lights in the school zone, but they have not worked properly since school began. I am not sure what time the school zone speed limit is actually in effect.

In the line with the rest of traffic, speeding through the school zone, I wonder if non-working flashing lights are an adequate legal defense for speeding through a school zone. That is concern for civil law. "What if I am found guilty?" The Law of the Lord has to do with respect for the One whose creation includes the creation of law. It has to do with concern for the purpose of the law, which is the safety of the children who are traveling to the school.

In Genesis we are taught that God is creator. In the New Testament we are taught that God is love. But the concept that God is law seems strange to our ears. The image of a "legal God" makes God stern, relentless, unyielding, unmerciful. But God's creation and love are known through the keeping of the law.

It means that the Law of God expressed in Scripture and to the degree embodied in society, is not a lifeless body of rules, but the living expression of God's will. God created a world where conduct counts. God created a world where the keeping of his Law revives the soul, makes wise the simple, rejoices the heart, enlightens the eyes, is to be more desired than gold and is sweeter than honey.

But that is not the common wisdom. Polls that give approval ratings of various professions generally rate attorneys about the same level as sellers of used cars. They defend guilty and innocent. But the polls do not reflect that. Police who are sworn to uphold the law can become objects of protest. Judges who manage the courts can bear the wrath of much anger.

Passion for the law is generally expressed when the law is broken, not when it is being kept. In Scripture the prophets passionately decry injustice when God's Law is broken. Keeping the law generally does not generate that kind of passion. But in this psalm there is passion for keeping the Law. The psalmist says that the reward for keeping the Law is to have the life which God's Law produces.

Common wisdom says that the best way to be refreshed is to go into God's creation. One Wednesday I was on a retreat way far out in the country. It was refreshing. I arrived early, drove around, saw a couple of deer running across the road. I got to walk through the path in the woods. That is one kind of refreshment. That is being in touch with one part of God's creation.

The psalmist says that keeping God's Law is another kind of refreshment of enormous value by itself. There is a joy in keeping God's commandments and ordinances regardless of what others do or what happens in the rest of the world.

One of my personal heroes is a television newscaster in Cleveland. When he was chosen the regular lead anchor on the weekday news, it was a promotion of note, since he was the first black to be a weekday news anchor in Cleveland. I always liked him. There was some quality about him, his manner, the way he treated others that I admired, but I didn't know what it was. Then one day, reading an interview with him, I discovered it.

When he talked about the advice that shaped his life, he said that his mother had told him no matter what anyone else did, he should always be a gentleman. He always followed that advice. Even if all around you are breaking the Laws of God and society, you know who you are and what you are to do.

That is the right kind of attitude: to do what is right regardless of anyone else's approval or disapproval, regardless of whether you are rewarded or punished at the time, regardless of what anyone else is doing, regardless of the popular behavior of the group you are with.

The last part of this psalm considers what happens when we do violate the Law of God. It asks a basic question: ". . . who can discern his errors?" How objective can we be about ourselves? How honest can we be with ourselves? How honest to God? How honest with others?

Out of our natural weakness the psalmist makes the petition, "Clear thou me from hidden faults. Keep back thy servant also from presumptuous sins; let them not have dominion over me!" The presumptuous sins are those which we commit because of the self-certainty we have of our judgment. Any one of us can rationalize a reason for murdering someone at whom we are angry. We can easily become confident of our reasoning.

That brings us to the eighth step: Made a list of all persons we had harmed, and became willing to make amends to them all. It is God's will that we keep the Law, and in keeping it is the joy the psalmist describes. To keep from breaking it and to become willing to make amends, we need to call on God's power to defend us from ourselves. It is to this need to be reconciled with God and one another that Paul wrote to the church in Corinth.

Knowing about the glory of keeping God's Law, and being aware of the need for and promise of reconciliation is a start, but there are some things that can keep us from being reconciled to God and one another. Sometimes we are just enjoying the wrong we are doing too much to really want to change.

Perhaps your prayer is that of Augustine who, early in life, prayed, "Give me chastity and self-control, but not just yet." He explained why he prayed this: "For I was afraid that you would hear my prayer too soon, and too soon would heal me from the disease of lust which I wanted satisfied rather than extinguished (*Confession,* VIII, 7.2)."

Sometimes we enjoy our sins too much to want to change. Other times, we feel so badly that we cannot believe God would really forgive us. Here is the promise of the gospel. God is "not counting (our) trespasses against (us) . . ." We are not locked in the prison of our misdeeds. We are free to go and be reconciled with those whom we have harmed.

This does not remove the consequences of our sins. If we poison the neighbor's dog, the dog is still dead. It does not remove the sin. It forgives the sinner.

The operative word in this section of Paul's letter is the word *reconciliation*. That is what this step is all about. "Made a list of all persons we had harmed, and became willing to make amends to them all."

That is a huge chore. But it is approachable because of what God has already done in Jesus Christ. We do not have to create reconciliation. We just have to follow the script that Christ wrote.

This is a step we can take only when we believe God has completely forgiven us. If we do not really believe we are forgiven, then we will not try to do this. This is a good litmus test of how fully you understand your forgiveness: how willing you are to make amends for the past? Forgiveness requires our acceptance. Acceptance is demonstrated in this step.

Last century two men named Wilson and Porter were sentenced in a federal court to be hanged. Two days before the hanging, President Andrew Jackson pardoned them both. But Wilson refused the pardon. That posed a complicated legal problem that ultimately reached the Supreme Court. They ruled:

"A pardon is a deed, to the validity of which delivery is not complete without acceptance. It may be rejected by the person to whom it is tenured, and if rejected, we have no power in this court to force it upon him."

If you knew that someone was coming by this afternoon to repossess your car, you probably would not stop on the way home and pay for it to be washed. You are more likely to run it through mud puddles and drive it through potholes.

If you do not feel you have been forgiven, then you will not try to clean up your act.

This is a secular way of saying that the old is passing away. This is a kind of programatic way of demonstrating to yourself the passing away of the old. If we make a decision to turn our will and way over to God, but we do not do anything differently, then the old ways still reign.

It also requires us to be ready to accept anyone and everyone whom we feel has wronged us. Paul talks about us being the "agents" of reconciliation. That is like being the manufacturer's representatives for God. A manufacturer's representative does not manufacture the product. He represents it. We do not manufacture reconciliation. God manufactures reconciliation. We let folks know about it. And that may well involve seeking reconciliation with someone you have harmed.

To the question, "Why do I forgive anyone?" Albert Schweitzer answered, "I must forgive the lies directed against myself because my own life has been so many times blotted by lies; I must forgive the lovelessness, the hatred, the slander, the fraud, the arrogance which I encounter since I myself have so often lacked love, hatred, slandered, defrauded and been arrogant (*Civilization and Ethics,* tr. John Naish, London: A&C Black, 1923, II, 260)."

No one said it was easy. That is why there are seven serious steps before it. It is the difficult and narrow way. But to be faithful to the gospel is to love the Law of God, the Law which Christ came not to remove but to fulfill. To be faithful to the gospel is not just to confess to God what is wrong in our life, but to get ready to let God use us as agents of reconciliation by making amends to any we have harmed.

STEP NINE — DISCIPLINE

Numbers 5:5-10
Ephesians 4:25-32
Matthew 5:21-26

Step nine: "Made direct amends to such people wherever possible, except when to do so would injure them or others."

In these passages of Scripture, we have rather specific advice. Let us look first at the Old Testament, the book of Numbers. The bulk of the Law is given in Exodus and Leviticus, and then again in Deuteronomy.

This morning's passage is a law of restitution, a special case law, supplemental to Leviticus 6:1-7. It deals with restitution in the situation in which there is no kinsman, that is, no living relative. Sometimes, even back then, litigation could go on for decades and the original plaintiff might be dead, along with all of the plaintiff's family. The advice is: give it to the temple. It is just like church trustees today who urge folks to leave it to the church.

There is nothing mentioned here about going to court. This is too for the person who was detected in dishonesty which he tried to conceal, got caught, went to court and was convicted. If the matter went to court, the consequences for the offender were more serious.

For example, Exodus 22:1 says, "If a man steals an ox or a sheep, and kills it or sells it, he shall pay five oxen for an ox, and four sheep for a sheep. He shall make restitution; if he has nothing, then he shall be sold for his theft. If the stolen beast is found alive in his possession, whether it is an ox or an ass or a sheep, he shall pay double."

This passage from Numbers is for one who chooses to avoid court, for the person whose conscience prompted him to make voluntary restitution. In addition to restoring to the person wronged the property plus one fifth of its value, the one seeking to make restitution was to present a ram to the sanctuary.

The reason for the offering to God is because we find time and again in Scripture that to wrong another is not simply to wrong another, it is to wrong God as well. To get things right with another is not simply to get things right with another, it is to get things right with God as well.

Again we find that injuring another is not simply a sin against that person. It is also a sin against God. Restitution must be made to that person, and restitution must be made to God.

The gospel lessons also deal with an issue of law. It sounds like Jesus is also suggesting that we settle out of court. He talks of an adversary who is going to speak against you in a lawsuit. And Jesus warns that if this goes to court you will have to pay to the very last coin.

There is some good advice here. If one accused has the wisdom to ingratiate himself to his accuser on the way to court, he can save himself a lot of legal expenses, and perhaps even some jail time.

Settling this without litigation also gives us the opportunity to take the initiative. The court case is adversarial. You go to court to have someone — be it a judge or jury — decide who is to blame. But Jesus urges us to go to the one from whom we are estranged without having to decide who is right or who is wrong. My neighbor may have something against me that I am quite justified in believing is not my fault. I can still take the initiative to get things right.

This is a message about religion and reconciliation. What if you are in church, and there start to think of the one with whom you are in conflict? It was the custom then to offer various gifts at the temple, from bulls and cows down to doves and offerings of incense, or, where it might be more convenient, an offering of money equivalent in value to these things. Jesus said, "If you are at the altar and there remember your brother has something against you, leave your offering there. First, go be reconciled with your brother or sister, then return to make the offering."

I just wondered what would happen if I refused to take the morning offering until everyone signed a pledge that they had been reconciled with all their adversaries. I believe I could have a lot of payless paydays. Our first priority may be to receive the offering. God's first priority is to remember our wrongs against another and to be reconciled.

If you are like me, your mind wanders a lot, often in church. One of my most embarrassing moments came during a wedding service. The couple had asked me to include the Lord's Prayer at the end of the wedding prayer. I remembered to start the prayer, but my mind wandered to what I was to do next. I forgot where we were in the Lord's Prayer.

This was a huge old church building and the people in the wedding party and the congregation were barely whispering the prayer. So when I knew I was lost, I tried to whisper softer than they did until I thought everyone else was done whispering. Then, in much embarrassment, I went on with the wedding service.

It is not a good idea for the worship leader to do that, but it can be a good thing when the minds of the worshipers begin to wander, depending on where they wander. "Going to the altar remember . . ." This should be a time of remembrance. Here is the place to remember both the need to be reconciled and God's great work of reconciliation.

Sometimes we remember things that can lead to litigation. Much more likely, what we remember is a relationship problem. There are a couple of things Jesus tells folks not to include in their conversations. The first is translated "anger," which describes a tone of voice that expresses contempt for another.

The second word is not easily translated. In English it is usually translated "fool." It is not an insult simply to someone's intelligence. This word was an insult to a person's character. If you have destroyed another's name and reputation, you are liable to the fires of Gehenna.

These fires are in the valley of Ben Hinnon. This is south-west of Jerusalem, where the evil King Ahaz introduced to Israel the fire worship of the god Molech, for whom little children were burned as a sacrifice (2 Chronicles 28:3).

Because of its evil reputation, it became the place where the garbage of Jerusalem was thrown, the public incinerator. In the peoples' minds this place became associated with all that was evil and filthy, a place where useless and evil things were destroyed by fire. If we try to destroy another's character, we are liable to ourselves be thrown on the refuse heap.

Most of us are not worried about serving time in jail or burning in the fires of hell. I remember my mother having written in a devotional booklet some reference to us "medium-size sinners." At Paul's conversion he could see very clearly what he was doing wrong. He was helping kill Christians. Most of us do not have sins that are so easy to define. Most of us keep within the letters of the law. It is the sins of the mind that are the falling of most of us.

Do you remember a couple of decades ago when people were arguing against proposed civil rights legislation? One of the arguments against it was, "You cannot legislate attitudes and morality." That is true. There are laws against murder, but not against hatred (unless you take for your rule of life what Jesus said).

Jesus said that he did not come to abolish the Law and the Prophets. Jesus did not come to abolish the laws regarding murder. Rather, he taught that our righteousness must exceed what is required. The Jewish teaching defined sin legalistically as consisting principally in the overt act. Jesus showed that God's law consists principally in the intention of the heart.

Murder begins with hostility or hatred. Such hostility makes us guilty before God, even though we are restrained from the actual act of violence. The evil desire within us is the root of the sin to which it can lead.

It is the attitude of the heart Jesus came to change, not just the outward action. Stop calling or thinking of your adversary as a blockhead. Stop saying things that hurt another's reputation. The change of heart becomes the change of action.

The Old Testament Book of Numbers gives us a guide on how to settle out of court in a way that gets things right both with the one wronged and with God. Jesus talked about the change of heart that exceeds and fulfills the law. Paul writes to the church about the behavior expected of Christians.

What are the qualifications to be a member of the church of Jesus Christ? What is expected of you and me? What behavior on our part is scandalous? Paul wrote this letter to the church folks in Ephesus. He assumed that church folks are equally tempted to lie, lose their temper, steal, and talk dirty. He must have assumed that we are people who can at times be characterized by bitterness, wrath, clamor, slander and malice.

The good news is Jesus did not come to call the righteous, but sinners to repentance. One part of the good news is that we do not have to pretend we are something we are not. God loves us as we are. The other part of the good news is that with God's help my life can be better.

This is not some religious idealism unconnected to our real world. The gospel is realistic. Anger is a common emotion, and one we can all understand. A capacity for anger is simply something God gave us.

The God of this Bible is a God who gets angry. The prophet Isaiah (54:8) brings us God's Words, saying, "In overflowing wrath for a moment I hid my face from you, but with everlasting love I will have compassion on you." As persons created in the image of God, we, too, get angry, but unlike God, we often lack the compassion to keep that anger from being destructive.

So Paul advises, "Be angry but do not sin, do not let the sun go down on your anger." Jesus and Paul seem here to conflict. Jesus said not to be angry. Paul said be angry, but do not sin. But in Greek there are two words for anger. One is *thumos,* which is described as being like the flame which comes from igniting dried straw. It blazes up, and just as quickly dies down.

The other word is *orge',* which is described as habitual anger. It is the long-lived anger that we nurse, just like we would nurse a fire we wanted to keep us warm all night. It is the anger we brood over and will not allow to die. This is the anger which refuses to be reconciled. This is the anger which insists on revenge.

Resentment and grudges have a way of becoming permanent if we let them fester. Do not nurse our anger, just in case it tries to go away. Again, Paul gives very practical advice. The day of your anger should be the day of your reconciliation. To be human is to get angry. To be humans created in the image of God is to have compassion and give the anger to God before we sin.

Ours is the gospel of reconciliation. Paul assures us that we are guilty of such things. We do not throw away people who have done wrong. If we threw away everyone here who had ever gotten angry, there would be no congregation, and certainly there would be no preacher.

Neither do we throw away the thief. Rather, we counsel as did Paul, "Let the thief no longer steal, but rather let him labor, doing honest work with his hands . . ."

It is the last part of that statement that I find remarkable. There has been a lot of talk about rehabilitating criminals to make them useful members of society. There is a lot of concern about the cost of keeping criminals in jail. We know about the anxiety it causes us when we worry about being victims of crime.

But Paul's concern is about reforming the thief, turning the thief into an honest worker, not to save society money, not to calm our anxieties about having our silver or stereos stolen. Paul's concern in reforming the thief is for this purpose: ". . . so that he may be able to give to those in need." The thief is transformed from a taker to a giver.

Paul talks about our emotions, our behavior, and our words. "Let no evil come out of your mouths, but only such as is good for edifying, as fits the occasion." What parent has not given that advice to their child? "Don't say bad words and don't lie. If you don't have anything good to say, don't say anything."

But again, listen to the purpose for which Paul says this: ". . . that (God's work) may impart grace to those who hear." There is an exemplary behavior expected of Christians, behavior which can make right the things that we and others have made wrong.

We are not just talking here about social graces. Any good book of social behavior will tell you, "Do not show bitterness, wrath, anger, clamor, slander and malice — in public." This is good advice on social propriety. We have not just been given the "what" of good behavior, but the "why." The "why" is the last part of that passage: ". . . as God in Christ has forgiven you."

It is by God's grace that we have the opportunity to make amends. It is by God's grace that we are allowed to be reconciled. Jesus said, "You have heard it said of old . . . but I say to you." Paul says, "Now therefore . . ." This is a new agenda, a new opportunity.

Jesus has been called the hinge of history. He is the point around which all turns. All of history is dated by that change — before Christ and after Christ. And so should a person's life have this kind of change point. That is both what Christ commanded and the amendment of life that Christ makes possible.

STEP TEN — PERSEVERENCE

Psalm 15:1-5
1 Corinthians 10:1-13
Luke 12:42-48

Step ten: "Continued to take personal inventory and when we were wrong, promptly admitted it." The 12 steps are a long journey, and the texts for today are ones that help us continue on the long journey.

This passage from Corinthians is one I think should be a history teacher's delight. It is a mode of scriptural interpretation known as "typology." It is a form of historical study. This method sees events in the history of Israel as "types" of events like other events. Here the redemptive events in Israel's history foreshadow and are similar to the final victory through Christ.

The past has lessons. Years ago my mother had me read these words: "Alas, times are not what they used to be. Children no longer obey their parents, and everyone wants to write a book about it." That was written in Egypt, about 2000 B.C. The types of events that happened before happen today.

Paul was using these lessons to speak to some church folk in Corinth who thought themselves protected by their baptism and communion despite their actions outside the church.

Paul then reminded them how the Hebrews traveled to the edge of the Red Sea, and though they were sure they had left Egypt only to die in the desert, God parted the sea, and they crossed safely while their pursuers entered the sea only to drown. Crossing the Red Sea and the enveloping cloud are "types" of Christian baptism. But that was no protection against the consequences of their behavior.

The miraculous good, the manna from heaven, and drink are "types" of the Lord's Supper. But that was no protection against the consequences of their behavior.

Paul refers to the wonderful statement in Exodus 13:21, telling about the people of Israel who were fleeing from the Pharaoh: "And the Lord went before them by day in a pillar of cloud to lead them along the way, and by night in a pillar of fire to give them light, that they might travel by day and night." But that miracle God gave them was no protection against the consequences of their behavior.

When they were thirsty, God told Moses to strike a rock with his rod, and water gushed forth. Rabbinic tradition says that the rock then followed them through the wilderness, a legend they would have known. According to Paul, the rock itself is a type of Christ. But that was no protection against the consequences of their behavior.

Baptism and partaking in the Lord's Supper are not enough to guarantee salvation, any more than it was a guarantee of salvation to go with Moses across the Red Sea or to be fed in the desert.

The people strayed after having been given such privilege by God. Twenty-three thousand who died in the wilderness were involved in both sexual immorality and idolotry. Many of the men became sexually involved with Moabite women and were drawn to the pagan altars by these women. It does not say having illicit sex killed them there and then. It did cause them to stay wandering in the desert the rest of their lives, no longer able to receive the promise.

Even those whose sin was complaining were struck down (Numbers 14:29-30). If you think it is okay to grumble, remember that all those who grumbled against God in the wilderness were refused entrance into the promised land. Even those blessed by such a great miracle were not protected from the consequences of their misdeed.

We may think all is well with God since we led a good life so far and God's favor has shown on us. Now we can coast a bit. But Paul warns, "Therefore let any one who thinks that he stands take heed lest he fall (10:2)."

There is a cartoon of a couple driving around, apparently lost, saying, "I know the church is around here somewhere. It was here last Easter." Many of us wait until there is a crisis to recall God's grace. "I know God's grace is around here somewhere. It was here last emergency."

Paul warns not to depend on the past and what those people did. That is no protection to us. It reminds me of the couple who came to see me because they wanted to get married.

After we exchanged names and shook hands, his opening statement was, "The first thing I want you to know is that my grandfather gave a lot of money to this church." Since he himself had no relationship with the church, I can only assume he wanted a cut-rate wedding. In the category of "What I should have said . . ." is, "What have you ever done for the church?"

The good deeds of those who went before us have no consequence for us. There was a major controversy in the early days of the church in this nation called the "Half Way Covenant."

The first generation of adults who settled in Massachusetts were confessing Christians, as were almost all of their children. But there came a time when some of the children drifted from the church. They, however, still wanted to come to the church for weddings, baptisms and funerals.

It was decided that if your parents were church members, you were entitled to the rites of the church. But a generation later it got stretched even further so that if your grandparents were church members, you were entitled to receive the rites of the church, even if neither you nor your parents were active believers.

Eventually they reexamined this "half way covenant" and came to realize the truth of what Paul said. It does not matter what your parents believe let alone your grandparents. We all face God alone. We must account to God alone.

The past teaches lessons. A feeling that all is now secure can be a terrible illusion. A woman chose to live in a maximum security building in Tulsa, Oklahoma, because it would feel safer from burglars and muggers. But the very security of the building cost her her life.

One night she became ill and called an ambulance. But the ambulance attendants could not get into the building because of security. When the police arrived, they could not get in to help her because of the security. When the apartment manager finally arrived, it was too late. The building security kept her from getting the life-saving help she needed.

We can put things around us — the good our parents did or the good we have done, the blessings we have received — and think all is secure.

Baptism does not make us safe. Receiving the Lord's Supper does not make us safe. What our parents did 30 years ago or what we did yesterday does not make us safe. Paul urges those of us who are self-confident to be vigilant. Do not sit back waiting for a miracle of God to take care of you.

We can be like that man who prayed and prayed that God would help him win the New York lottery. He had been a good man. Certainly he had great and legitimate needs. Somebody was going to win the lottery, why not him? So he prayed night after night, "Dear God, please let me win the lotteory." After months and months of praying with no answer, in great frustration he finally asked God why his prayers had not been answered. There came a voice from heaven saying, "Give me a chance. At least buy a ticket!"

The promise is not for those who sit and wait for God to take care of their needs. It is for those who with perseverence face life's trials.

Paul tells us that God gives us what we need to face life. Whatever the day brings, we can face it. Any temptation that comes to us is not unique. Others have endured it and others have come through it. When we are going through things, we are going through things others have, by the grace of God, suffered, endured and conquered.

The purpose of a test is not to make the student fail, but to emerge stronger than ever. We are not delivered from temptation, but we are promised the strength to face it, and to grow because we faced it.

Paul does not say that it is God who tempts us, but God who permits the temptation. It is like the petition in the Lord's Prayer: "lead us not into temptation." God allows the test and gives us a way to pass the test, to be led from temptation. God will not allow us to be subjected to an impossible strain.

None of this negates any of the benefits of being baptized and receiving the Lord's Supper. It puts it in proper perspective. We are given entry into the life of faith. We are given sustenance to live the life of faith. It is for us to be vigilant and persistent.

Vigilance and persistence are also the message of Jesus' parable of the faithful and unfaithful servants. Why the unfaithfulness? There was a delay which led to the freedom to act without the thought of consequences.

I think this is the lesson for the presidential candidate and the television preacher whose misdeeds are exposed in the media. Most of us have done things of which we are not proud. We did what we thought at the time seemed the thing to do. We were not thinking about some divine judgment exposing what we were doing.

That glare of publicity that the politician and television preacher receive is something like what happens in God's judgment. All the secret sins are no longer secret but known to the point of excruciating embarrassment. The judgment does not kill you, but causes the deepest pain. The very shame is punishment enough.

Even seeing ourselves growing spiritually and emotionally can cause problems. Most of us can look back at our lives and feel good about significant accomplishments we have made along the way. There are certain temptations we have overcome. There are bad habits we have corrected. There are emotions we can now at last control.

We may feel rightly that we have something about which to feel good. It has been a long, difficult journey, so we are going to coast. If I knew the judgment were coming today, I would get ready. But it has been so long delayed, I am going to rest a bit. I will take some time off from what I know is right. But God does not let us get away with that so easily.

We have a wonderful, awful burden. We have heard the warning of Paul. We know what is required. We have heard the gospel read. We know what is required. We have heard Psalm 15 read. We know what is required. Therefore more is required of us than if we had not heard, and the failure to obey bears more serious consequences.

It is Psalm 15 that specifically talks about the things God requires of us. The psalm is addressed to the sojourner, the permanent guest. This is like the theme we have chosen for our church stewardship campaign this fall: This is not my church, this is not your church. This is God's church. We are the guests. What qualifies us to be a guest in God's house? The psalmist asked, "Who is qualified to dwell in fellowship with God?"

This particular psalm is referred to as a liturgy for admission to the temple. "Liturgy" is a term which refers to the order of worship. Literally it means "the work of the people." This lists the work the people need to do to be worthy to worship God.

Think of this as a psalm that would be read responsively. The people ask, "Who shall sojourn in thy tent? Who shall dwell on the holy hill?" The priest answers with a listing of 10 commandments.

— *he who walks blamelessly, and does what is right,*
— *and speaks the truth from his heart;*
— *who does not slander with his tongue,*
— *and does no evil to his friend,*
— *nor spreads rumors about his neighbor;*
— *who despises those whom God rejects,*
— *but who honors those who fear the Lord;*
— *who swears to his own hurt and does not change;*
— *who does not put out his money at interest,*
— *and does not take a bribe against the innocent.*

As we find elsewhere in this series, worthiness of worship in God's house has very much to do with how we treat God's people. The conclusion of the psalm is that doing what is required is to receive this blessing: "He who does these things shall never be moved."

Life is a long journey, and on a long journey we get tired. We need to be fed and renewed. For those who seek to be faithful in the journey, whether they follow the 12 steps of AA, the 10 listed in the psalm, or another particular journey of faith, is what kept the faithful people going for 40 years through the desert with Moses, what kept Paul going through his trials, is what can help us gain strength, the place where faith is to be built, which is Christ, our solid rock.

STEP ELEVEN — SPIRITUALITY

Psalm 25:1-15
1 Thessalonians 5:12-22
Matthew 26:36-46

This past week I had a new adventure. I did some plumbing work I had never done before. But I got out my handy homeowner's guide, and followed along step by step. It took longer than I thought it would. But at last it was almost complete. Close to the very end came the time when I put on the nuts and bolts that held it all together.

As we reach toward the end of this series, we are approaching the step that tightens down and holds in place all the other work. The 11th step is: "Sought through prayer and meditation to improve our conscious contact with God, as we understood him, praying only for knowledge of his will for us and the power to carry that out."

The 25th Psalm was written by one trying to get his life together. This is the psalm of someone who has taken a long, hard look at his life and decided something has been seriously wrong and something much better is possible, both because of what he is willing to do, and because of what God is willing to permit.

Some consider this the psalm of the medium-sized sinner. It does not appear that there was necessarily some terrible crisis that occurred. But the moment sometimes comes without any particular crisis when we are ready to take a long look at our lives, turn everything over to God, trust in his leading, and try to move toward that newness of life.

The image in this psalm of God plucking our feet out of the net is one worth exploring. This net would be the one hunters used then to catch wild animals. They would dig a hole along the path an animal would take to get to their drinking place. Is this not an appropriate image for this series? The hole would be covered over, the animal would drop in, and there would be the net to catch hold of it.

The more it struggles to get out, the more it becomes entangled. The plea is for God to help get us out of this tangled net. Maybe we got caught up on the way to the drinking place, or somewhere else we may have gone out of habit, probably innocently. But we got tangled up, and the more we struggled on our own, the worse it got. The psalmist is trying to strike a deal with God to get him out of what he has gotten caught in.

Recall Jacob's dream at Bethel, and how Jacob tried to bargain with God. Jacob said that if God would give him clothes and food, and see that he got home safely, then this God would become his God. That hardly seems a mature religious concept. But God let him bargain. Here is another bargain. The psalmist promises certain things, like trusting God, waiting for God, watching for God.

In exchange, he asks God not to let him be put to shame, not to let his enemies exalt over him, to teach him God's truth, to be merciful, to remember God's covenant love, and then asks God to forget the sins of his youth. It is a prayer that, like all good prayers, involves baring our souls to God.

There is no particular order to the verses in the psalm. What he was doing was having each verse begin with another letter of the Hebrew alphabet. Their sequence has no particular significance to us. But some sections are particularly worth a second look.

He does seem to have had a serious problem with some people he identified as his enemies. In good measure this psalm is a prayer of deliverance from personal enemies. We are taught by Jesus to pray for our enemies. It is also right and proper to pray for deliverance from our enemies.

"Let not my enemies exalt over me." There are people whose presence in our thinking can continue to trouble us. There may be people you do not want to see because they have a better position, higher salary, the lover you wanted, the athletic ability you covet. You cannot stand the thought of their being smug about it.

Maybe they would have a malicious interest in your problems. You can just see their smirks, you can hear their mocking laughter. The psalmist does not ask God to destroy them. It is more the prayer of one who wants to be released from the torment which thoughts of them bring. "Release me from concern about whatever my enemies might think or do or say." That is a healthy prayer.

He recognizes his enemies and the troubles they have caused him, but he does not blame them for his troubles. I chose the path I took. If I fall into the net on this path, it is my responsibility.

In the midst of his trial the psalmist seeks "to know" God's will for him. This word translated "to know" is not a kind of academic knowledge, like knowing the number for *pi*. It is "knowing" in the same way a husband and wife know each other, the same kind of intimacy. It is moving from what we learn in the reading and hearing of Scripture to having that in our inner being. We are talking about God's will for us.

When a lot of people talk about "God's will" it makes me nervous. When the psalmist wrote this, he did not have in mind some great computer chip in the sky with my name and program all printed out. If you work with computers, you know that hitting the wrong button can completely destroy a program. If you lose power for just an instant, all the information you have just programmed can be lost. But if you hit the right buttons and do not lose power, the computer can do amazing things. God cannot be thought of like that. There are no programs laid out for us like AAA will plan our trips with all the routes and exits marked.

Especially when trouble strikes, I have a lot of difficulty calling that God's will. I do not think it is God's will that people are killed in war or that school buses fall off cliffs. I do not believe it is fair to say that the tragedy is God's will, but in the midst of that tragedy there are things God wills to have happen.

It is the difference between saying that it is God's will that a house catches fire, and saying that "if" the house catches fire, God's will is for it to be extinguished and the people gotten out safely. It is not God's will that our enemies exult over us. But if our enemies do what ought not to be done, then in that situation God has a will and a way for us to follow.

Doing God's will is not first having a road map. It is first trusting in what we will not see this side of eternity. The psalmist was mindful of God's steadfast will from of old (v. 6) and trusted that day because of what God has done in the past.

The will of God is not simply something that happens to us. The will of God is something to do. It involves our being willing to pray for knowledge and to pray for the strength to carry out that will.

The psalm is a plea for personal help. Paul pleads for the kind of community which helps those who are struggling with life's direction. Paul was not writing to a prosperous church. He was writing to a new church that had struggled and was about to enter into a far more difficult struggle. He was writing to a church where many within the fellowship were struggling with their life and faith.

Like the psalmist, Paul gives us a whole catalogue of things to consider in the life of faith. Our concerns are often like the Psalmist's; worries about our enemies, about our children, about the sins of our youth, about our relationship to God.

But sometimes our life's journey is not primarily asking God to help us, but to agonize with God for people whose lives are troubled. It is in loving one another, loving the unlovely and the unlovable, loving the fainthearted and spiritually frail, loving those caught up in a snare, that our journey of faith reaches outward.

There are some of us who are easily discouraged, those who are the "faint-hearted." The weak to whom Paul refers were possibly a morally unstable group, people still caught up in their sins. Paul urges the church to (21) "test everything; hold fast to that which is good."

One of the reasons the psalmist mentioned youth is that is often the time when we test everything. Limits get tested: how fast to drive, how far to go sexually, how daring in trying drink and drugs, how much to cheat on tests. Our is not to repay people with evil for the evil they have done. Ours is not to quench the spirit. Ours is to help the weak, to be patient with all persons.

Paul gives what seems rosy advice "Rejoice always." Why? Should we really be giving thanks to God for all the struggles of life? Should the alcoholic really give thanks for the struggle with addiction? Should the epileptic really give thanks for the continued silent threat? Should the childless couple really give thanks for infertility? Should the chronically depressed really give thanks for their depression? The list of painful questions is endless.

I do not give thanks for the struggle of the soul when I find myself praying as Jesus did in the garden, "Let this cup of suffering pass from me." That seems an inhuman choice to have to make.

But notice that Paul did not say be thankful for everything but in every circumstance. I was not thankful that my mother died of cancer. But in that circumstance I was thankful: thankful for the comfort of the Holy Spirit; thankful for the strength my mother received from her prayers and the prayers of others, thankful for the love and support my mother received from family and friends; thankful for the church's continuing ministry to her.

There are those who think that the words "religion" and "rejoicing" do not belong together.There are a lot of people who think that if something is fun, it cannot be Christian. "Everything I like is either illegal, immoral or fattening." We have a joy that is deeper than an immediate pleasure.

We rejoice when we know that the grips of the old way of living have been broken. We rejoice when people have been released from the nets that held them. We rejoice when peoples' lives are transformed by the renewal of their mind. Christ's life embodied that deeper joy.

In the life of Jesus we have one who both prayed for himself to understand and to do God's will, and who in love reached out to pray for others, that they would also know and do God's will. Let me set the scene for the gospel reading. That night Jesus celebrated his last supper with his disciples. If you recall, they did have wine with supper, and sometimes when things get tense we like just a bit of the grape to help us relax and rest.

Remember also that there were arguments at the last supper. For most of the people most of the time, a glass of wine will help you relax and become more social. But for others it has the opposite effect. It causes them to become belligerent and anti-social. One of the effects of excessive consumption of alcohol is the suppression of our capacity to reason and the suppression of the basic moral standards we have developed.

Do you remember the song from "Jesus Christ Superstar," which is a kind of irreverent song the disciples sang after their last supper with Christ? It portrays them as having gotten drunk, and being drunk, they lost the understanding of the gravity of the situation as Jesus had explained it, and started singing about retiring and writing the gospels.

The Bible commentaries do not talk about it, and the Bible does not specifically mention it, but it is entirely possible that Peter could not pray with Jesus because Peter had too much to drink and could not stay awake. This took place, after all, in an olive orchard.

If we are seeking to improve our conscious contact with God, praying only for knowledge of his will for us and the power to carry that out, periods of unconsciousness due to excessive consumption of alcohol and drugs is, at best, counterproductive.

So we have the scene in which Jesus struggles in prayer, and in his prayer we see how it can be terribly difficult to give your will to God. You know how difficult it can be for a child to do a parent's will, even if that is something so simple as putting away a jacket. Jesus struggled with his human will as it conflicted with God's will. He sought both the knowledge of what God wanted him to do, and the power to do it.

It is important to note that even though Peter was to fall asleep, one as great as the Son of the living God, sought out companionship with Peter in the hour of struggle. This should be an example to us to be willing to be with those who seek our help, and to be willing to seek others who ask us to help them face their trials.

Notice also that Jesus was concerned for Peter's capacity to know God's will and have the power to do that. Jesus wanted Peter to pray for himself. It was Jesus who was to face the betrayal, the trial, the beating and death. But Jesus wanted Peter to pray for himself, so that Peter would receive the power from God to face the time. Instead of praying, Peter slept.

Sleep is a great escape. That is part of the appeal in the use of drugs and alcohol. They make us, in the words of the song by Pink Floyd "comfortably numb." My best friend is about to get the axe. I cannot stand by and watch it happen. I will sit down, have a drink and become oblivious to all the pain.

I was listening to a radio talk show this week in which there was a discussion about adjusting to divorce. One woman called and voiced what is a common complaint. When she and her husband got divorced, she lost all her friends. Most people cannot bear to watch friends have such troubles, so they simply stop seeing them.

We can go to God for the strength to face the troubles and to receive the knowledge of what to do, because even if we are like Peter, turning our back on our best friend, perhaps having too much to drink and escaping into sleep when we should be on our knees praying passionately, God's greatest desire is to give us the strength we need.

There is a medieval legend which says that sometime during the 12th century, Henry II of England laid siege to the French city of Le Mans, but he failed to take it, and so he retired, baffled and enraged. According to the legend, he deliberately blasphemed God in order to ensure his own damnation. "Since thou hast taken from me the thing I most delight in — Le Mans — I will deprive thee of the thing thou hast most delight in — my soul."

The most painful thing to God is not our sins. It is most painful to God if we choose to let our sins keep us from God. It is the soul of each of us God cares for most passionately. Whether we are the weak, the idle, the fainthearted, our God waits to give us understanding and power, if we are only willing to seek earnestly it in meditation and prayer.

STEP TWELVE — RESPONSIBILITY

Isaiah 61:1-4
Galatians 6:1-10
Luke 19:1-10

Step 12: "Having had a spiritual awakening as the result of these steps, we tried to carry this message to others, and to practice these principles in all our affairs."

This is not a step inward in our own journey of life and faith. It is a step outward which we take after we have recognized where God has led us in this journey. It is, in religious language, the call of the missionary. It is the call to share the good news. For some it is the good news found in sobriety. But it is a step for anyone caught in any trap in life, who has been set free by the redeeming power of God.

This message is at the core of Scripture: The prophet Isaiah spoke the great words of promise to an ancient people. The gospel lesson tells of the joy felt by Zacchaeus when he who was lost became a new person. It is Paul who writes to the church with advice how we as individuals and as a church should act in carrying the good news to others.

As you study this letter to the church in Galatia, it appears that news reached Paul of some harsh judgment against one of the church members. There is no indication of what they had done wrong. The details of someone else's failure was not important to Paul, nor should it be to us.

What was of concern to Paul, however, was how those who have received the good news should relate to others. Our goal is not to cut off the offending member, but to bring healing. When I broke my ankle four years ago, I did not want to have it removed, but healed. So we should treat other members of the household of faith.

To hold ourselves up in pride over another is wrong. The Christian should never take the failure of another as an opportunity for self-congratulations. As Paul wrote to the church in Corinth: "Do not rejoice at the wrong, but rejoice at the right." The prophet Ezekiel wrote these words of God: "I take no delight at the death of the wicked, but that the wicked might turn from his way and live."

Paul was aware that some folks were doing things they should not be doing. There is no question about that. But Paul views these sins in a rather passive way. Those in question were not blatant and deliberate in what they did. The sinner did not plan to go out and sin. The sinner, in Paul's words, was "overtaken."

There are "sins" like alcoholism which are not deliberate sins. No one says, "When I grow up I want to be an alcoholic." "I know what will be fun. I'll spend my life lying and then covering up for my lies." "Here's a great career. I think I will spend the rest of my life making friends with people who will get me into trouble."

Sometimes in our sins we simply get caught up. We do not mean to do it. An illness overtakes us. The alcoholic reaches out to destroy others. He does not mean to. But he is no longer in control. It is like a swimmer who is drowning. The controls get anesthetized. You are just grasping for something to hold. You were trying to pull yourself up, but ended up dragging another down. In this situation you are overtaken.

There are sins we fall into because we simply are not in control of our lives. So those who know the good news that will set them free do not need to load people down with a greater sense of guilt and shame. We need to help people become unburdened.

"Come to me all you who labor and are heavy laden, and I will give you rest." We do not need to give the heavy laden more burdens.

Paul's words were a message to care-givers. His first message in this passage is: "Do not seek to condemn. Seek to restore. We are to be God's agents in helping to restore others.

We are, to use Paul's words in this text, to bear one another's burdens. Paul talks twice in this passage about bearing burdens, and what he says in these two places may seem contradictory.

First Paul says, "Bear one another's burdens, and so fulfill the law of Christ." We are to help one another. Then he says, "For each person will have to bear his own load." We are each expected to carry our own burden. How can it be both ways?

It has to do with helping another without expecting them to do the same. It is issuing a dinner invitation without expecting you will have the favor returned. It has to do with giving and not counting the cost. It has to do with the simple joy of helping others.

It has to do with helping others, but not helping to the point where they are never allowed to develop their own strength. We all need to bear our own burden as much as we can with the strength God supplied. It has to do with gaining strength as others help us bear our burdens.

It is like weight lifters. They constantly struggle to lift weights beyond their capacity. As they gain strength, they have someone with them helping to bear up the weight in case it gets too much, because to drop it would be disaster.

It has to do with being willing to bear one another's burdens, but not to eliminate one another's responsibilities. The calling of the church is to help those who get caught up to bear their burdens while God gives them strength.

It is very easy for the caregiver to become the careneeder. Back in the 1960s one of the "in" things for clergy was to have what was referred to as a "specialized ministry," such as an airport ministry, a shopping mall ministry, etc. A friend of mine developed a bar ministry. It worked for a while until he himself had a bit too much of the poison and had to take the treatment. We easily become the wounded healer.

Paul expresses a special concern for the caregiver. "Do good . . . especially to those of the household of faith." By itself that message is troublesome. Aren't we supposed to live for others and give to others? Isn't that what the church is about, going forth into the world in Christ's name?

The reason to give priority for the needs of church folks is not because God loves us any more than anyone else. But the caregivers must be cared for. When our fortunes shift, we can easily become the walking wounded.

As an analogy, Paul talks about the harvest. The apple farmer cannot just show up one fine day in October and pick the fruit off the trees. After the picking is done there is time to prune the trees. There is time to maintain and repair equipment. There is time to spray for bugs and disease, then it is time to prune all over again.

Paul urges us to be faithful in season — when the fruit is ready for picking — and out of season — when we see no bud and all we are doing is maintenance. Be faithful in our work even when there is no fruit seen on the tree.

Here we are urged to be faithful in sharing God's good news with the world. "Having had a spiritual awakening we tried to carry this message to others, and to practice these principles in all our affairs."

There are three images that come to mind. One involves fishermen. I remember someone telling me about going on a fishing trip somewhere and along the way meeting a group of other people out fishing. When he tried to engage these other people in conversation, they were silent. It seems that they were afraid that he was trying to find the location of their special fishing place. They were unwilling to share the good news.

The other image comes from the great church leader D.T. Niles. He said that evangelism is one beggar telling another beggar where to get food. For a long time I did not like that image. We are not beggars. But the more I thought about it, the more it makes sense to me.

If we believe what Scripture tells us, that none of us are worthy of God's love and grace, that life itself is a gift, that Christ's redemption of each of us is the ultimate gift, then it makes a lot of sense. We were given the gift of life. It cost us nothing. When we strayed, it was God who paid the price to redeem us. All we can do, then, as an act of gratitude, is to let others know where they, too, can receive this gift of life.

The third image comes from an incident that happened at a banquet I attended this past year. The banquet was held at one of the big downtown hotels that was hosting several other events that night. The hostesses for the banquet were members of the Ray of Hope Christian Church. When it came time for them to begin their hostess work, they had scattered throughout the entire floor of the hotel. So their pastor, in a loud voice, shouted: "Ray of Hope." Heads turned from all over, wondering what this ray of hope was. We know what the ray of hope is, and we are called to bring that ray of hope to an uncertain world.